D1291785

LABYRINTHS

LABYRINTHS

WALKING TOWARD THE CENTER

Gernot Candolini

Translated by Peter Heinegg

Foreword by Paula D'Arcy

A Crossroad Book
The Crossroad Publishing Company
New York

The Crossroad Publishing Company
481 Eighth Avenue, New York, NY 10001

First published as *Im Labyrinth sich selbst entdecken,* copyright © Verlag Herder, Freiburg im Breisgau, 2001.

English translation copyright © 2003 by The Crossroad Publishing Company.

Printed in the United States of America

This book is set in 11/13.5 Triplex Serif Light. The display type is Triplex Serif Bold.

Library of Congress Cataloging-in-Publication Data

Candolini, G. (Gernot)
    [Im Labyrinth sich selbst entdecken. English]
    Labyrinths / Gernot Candolini ; translated by Peter Heinegg.
      p. cm.
    Includes bibliographical references.
    ISBN 0-8245-2102-1 (alk. paper)
    1. Labyrinths. I. Title.
    BL325.L3C3613 2003
    291.3'7 — dc21

                            2003011461

1 2 3 4 5 6 7 8 9 10   10 09 08 07 06 05 04 03

Contents

Foreword by Paula D'Arcy   7

Preface   11

1. Setting Out into a World of Mystery   13

2. The Angel's Smile   18

3. The Wonder of Gothic   21

4. Turnings   24

5. Paths in the Grass   27

6. In Hedgerows and Deserts   30

7. It's a Long Way   34

8. What You Learn with Your Feet   38

9. Map of the Soul   44

10. The First Step   47

11. The Monster in the Mirror   50

12. Mother Earth   52

13. No Time for the Path   55

14. The Pearl   58

15. Paths of Pilgrimage   61

16. Just at the Point of Giving Up   64

17. Closing Circles   68

18. The First Construction   72

19.	The Sunwheel	76
20.	The Archive in Basel	80
21.	The Trip to Chartres	83
22.	The Navel of the World	87
23.	A Trip through the Ages	92
24.	Just Get It Right	95
25.	The Limits of Words	98
26.	Absolutely Certain	101
27.	The Wheel of Fire	105
28.	The Voice of the Heart	109
29.	The Path Back	112
30.	Labyrinthine Tales	116
31.	Precious Things Come Slowly	120
32.	Doubts about One's Own Path	123
33.	The Face of the Minotaur	126
34.	Turn Around or You're Trapped	129
35.	Discovering Oneself in the Labyrinth	132
36.	The Labyrinth Is a Mirror	135
37.	Good Questions Are Better Than Good Answers	139
38.	An Archetypal Image of Life	141
List of Illustrations		143
About the Author		144

Foreword

My introduction to Gernot Candolini was an air mail missive from him in November 2001 inviting me to be the guest speaker for a retreat to be held in an old farmhouse in Tuscany the following summer. Although we would gather in Italy for the retreat, the participants would all be Austrian, and the request was for me to speak about the male and female journeys. I said yes, knowing very little about what I was stepping into. The plan was for me to fly first to Innsbruck, Austria, where Gernot lived. There I would acclimate myself to European time and begin to know Gernot, who would only be my first taste of a team of four men with whom I'd work in Tuscany. My initial meeting of Gernot was shocking. During our months of correspondence, I had for some reason believed that Gernot was a woman's name. Adjusting to jet lag was secondary to adjusting to Gernot's gender! I still smile, remembering.

At Gernot's encouragement I explored Innsbruck in a lazy, unhurried way. I had lived there as a student some thirty years before, so it was both exploration and reunion. In the evenings I met with Gernot and his family. The richness of this man became slowly apparent. A fellow author, a photographer, biology teacher, husband, devoted father, engaging and deep thinker, and then, what I never anticipated, an international architect of labyrinths. So one afternoon I walked away from Innsbruck's colorful Old Town, and found my way to a city park where one of Gernot's labyrinths was waiting. Tucked into the heart of this sprawling park, carefully situated apart from the children's playground and a network of wide, inviting walking paths, was a labyrinth whose spirals were composed only of flowers...beautiful beds of yellow radiance. Nice. I entered the path of flowers and began to walk. And there at the center, when I arrived, was a reflecting glass. I remembered Gernot's words from the evening before, "In the labyrinth you discover yourself." It was a perfect beginning for the experience we were all about to share.

I met the entire team when we arrived in Tuscany, and they immediately and easily included me in their adventure of faith, trust, and friendship — a camaraderie these men had been nurturing for over twenty years. Within the first hours I knew that this experience mattered; that together we would create something extraordinary.

During the Tuscany retreat, we built two labyrinths. One, on a hilltop, was created from clay roof tiles. Another, in a stone chapel, was totally ringed with glittering tea lights. But it was Gernot's teachings that lead us. "Ask questions," he'd say. "Ask, what waits for me in the middle? What do I meet, deep in my soul? Do I move on? Do I follow the path? There's no right, no wrong. Just being on the way. Just keep walking. Think about what you'd like to risk in this lifetime. The path will offer everything you need. Walk, and look within."

Eight days later, when we bundled into a small European car to begin the long drive from Tuscany back to Innsbruck, my heart was more than full. Fellow team member Hubert was asleep in the back seat. Gernot was driving, and the manuscript for this book (in the original German) was spread across my lap. I turned the pages slowly, savoring words. I had forgotten my next day's early morning flight, or the pilgrimage Gernot would be leading that same morning. I read and we talked. Hours into the ride, and deep in conversation, Gernot suddenly cried out in alarm. I couldn't imagine what was wrong. At last he blurted out, "We missed our exit." Okay, I thought, but how terrible could that be? Then I learned how terrible. We'd missed the exit a full two hours before, and correcting the error would add four hours to a trip that was already nine hours long. Yet, looming ahead was the unmistakable proof: a sign reading, "Welcome to Milan."

But it was the moment that followed that caused me to see the fabric and fiber of Gernot Candolini. He looked at me, shook his head, and suddenly laughed. "Hubert," he called, "wake up!" When I seemed puzzled, he grinned. "I've heard," he said, light dancing in his eyes, "that the cathedral in Milan is not to be missed!" And that is how I happened to spend a surprising and wonderful afternoon in Milan, Italy, walking through the amazing cathedral there as if I had no early flight the next morning, and as if there were no other moment than the one before me. The cathedral had appeared on our path. We paid attention.

"This is the day that lies before you," Gernot had prayed with us each morning in Tuscany. "These are the hours. How will you meet them?" I'm aware that those same hours lie, like this book, in front of you. I hope you can give yourself to these pages, and to this extraordinary guide. Labyrinths can be walked not only with feet, but with hands and hearts and minds. Fall into the experience. These pages are a rich, wondrous blend of history, faith's deep call, and the wisdom gleaned from the journey. Gernot's path is simply, compellingly told. You won't be able to read quickly; some insights will cause you to ponder for a long while. Find your own pace. As you walk, listen to your own journey through his. The stories weave a certain magic. Pay attention.

"On a path two great crises await you. The first comes when the magic of the beginning has vanished. The second comes just before the goal. Both ask the question: Do you really want this?"
(from the text)

Paula D'Arcy

May 2003

Preface

I never cease to be amazed at the twists and turns life takes.

Wanted or not, the path one is on keeps changing.

Ever since I first happened across the labyrinth, my fascination with it has grown. Initially all I wanted was to have some quick questions about the labyrinth answered. Now I sometimes wonder if I'll ever return from this long trip to the information desk.

There's so much to discover in this apparently primordial symbol. It reveals so much about ourselves and others and the way of the world.

I'm grateful to my wife, Ulli, and my daughter, Hannah, for setting out with me on this journey of discovery, both of the history of labyrinths and of the labyrinth that is my own life.

Writing this book has been a great joy. In it, I share the stories of our travels by camper to numerous labyrinth sites in Europe, along with the insights that slowly grow through these personal encounters with the labyrinth.

The labyrinth is an image of life, a mirror of the soul, a symbol of humanity. Much lies waiting to be discovered in it. Above all waits oneself.

Gernot Candolini
Innsbruck

1

Setting Out into a World of Mystery

The Classical Labyrinth

*Life is a
constant traveling
in the labyrinth,
arriving
and moving on,
finding one's way to the center
and then leaving it,
having to turn but proceeding
into the path ahead.*

This is the only real night of cold in our long strange journey. Frost settles on windowpanes, meadows, and trees. We have parked our trailer on a side street under dark trees, settling in for the night alongside a few other trailers. They belong to circus people, who have set up tents farther back off the road in a park. The evening chill is uncomfortable but our moods are high. We're enjoying the hum of the gas heater, savoring it all the more for knowing how close I had come to not having it fixed before we left. The three of us are drawn close this first night in the tension felt by those embarking together on an adventure.

My wife Ulli and I had recently quit our jobs and given up our apartment, and didn't bother to look for new ones. We stored all our worldly goods in a garage and borrowed a trailer. Our daughter Hannah, not quite two years old, promises to be a wonderful traveling companion. We have no fixed itinerary and no defined goal for this journey, just plenty of time.

The first steps on our path have led us westward to France. On this cold night we have stopped with our circus neighbors, in a little village in the Champagne region. Hannah falls right to sleep. After Ulli and I clear the table we open our book. This book is our only guide: a compendium of the world's labyrinths.

My first encounter with the labyrinth was casual; a photo of one briefly captured my attention as I flipped through a picture calendar somewhere. Obviously its images made a strong impression on me.

Some time later I was walking through the garden of a health resort discussing landscaping possibilities with the director. We were absorbed in plans for installing a new path, when he abruptly asked me:

"And what could be built here?"

To my surprise, I spontaneously blurted out:

"A labyrinth."

"What's that supposed to mean?"

"I don't know, but I'll look into it."

And so I did, checking first on my local bookstore's website for books available on the subject. The printout I took from my computer held the first of many surprising discoveries. There on the list of books was a title, *Through the Labyrinth: Designs and Meanings Over 5,000 Years* by Herman Kern. I had expected this to be a simple research topic, certainly not something involving a five-thousand-year-history and full of meanings. The book description spoke of the labyrinth as a "archetype." What on earth did that term mean, anyway? At that moment I felt as if I'd found a door behind which lay a fascinating and mysterious world. I was captivated and decided to open the door.

I took a day off and drove to Vienna. In a little bookstore behind St. Stephen's cathedral the salesman pulled down the last copy of a big book of labyrinths from the top shelf.

I've always been fascinated by ancient cultures — the Egyptians, the Mayans, the Incas. So much about them defies modern explanation. My grandfather had often told me the story of the British archaeologist Howard Carter's discovery of Tutankhamen, and about Heinrich Schliemann's discovery of Troy. Like many boys and girls I dreamt that one day I too could discover a treasure, a mystery. From the very first the labyrinth awakened in me the joy of the discoverer, the one who sets out to seek his own treasure.

When I first opened the book, I was astonished to find how far from my conception was the world that lay behind this simple figure of the labyrinth. In my mind, the word "labyrinth" was associated with a picture of a maze of hedges next to some castle. But this notion was evidently only a small part of the whole story. Labyrinths, my reading told me, are something else — and only marginally related to mazes.

Most fundamentally, the labyrinth is a graphic figure constructed according to a definite rule. The rule is simple, and anyone who knows it can easily sketch a labyrinth. First you draw a cross, then four corners and a point in each one of them. Then the arms of the cross and the corners and points are connected seriatim with one another so as to form a circle. This creates an intertwined figure with an entrance and a center. A single path is created leading from the entrance to the center. The path encircles the center a total of seven times before reaching it. This path has neither dead ends nor turnoffs. Thus it's a path on which you can't get lost. But then what's a labyrinth good for?

In the course of history the labyrinth is found on silver coins, vases, pottery shards, and gold rings, scratched on rocks and laid out with stones. It shows up in countless far-flung cultures: among Cretans and Spaniards, Etruscans and Britons, Normans and American Indians, Hindus and Indonesians. Because the method of constructing it is so clear and, once grasped, so simple, the labyrinth hasn't changed for millennia. Hence this labyrinth has also been labeled the "classical labyrinth."

This is the labyrinth associated with the legend of Theseus: the place in Crete where the Greek hero conquered the Minotaur, which is why it is also known as the "Cretan labyrinth."

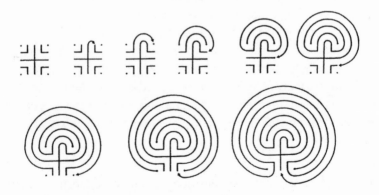

16

In the story of Theseus the labyrinth is not just the prison of the Minotaur. It makes a second appearance: when Theseus leaves Crete, he stops on the island of Delos. There he dances the *geranos* and the Crane dance with the freed hostages, following with their steps the lines of the labyrinth. So did the labyrinth also function as a dancing ground carved or sketched out in the ground?

2

The Angel's Smile

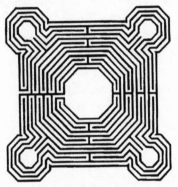

The former labyrinth
in the cathedral of Reims, France

*If there is a smile
at the beginning of a path,
then you'll find one
at the end as well.*

We're somewhere in the Champagne region of France. The trailer floor is cold, the gas heater is rumbling. Hannah has fallen asleep. We're studying the chapter "Church Labyrinths" in the book on our table. Tomorrow, we want to go to Reims, about sixty miles east of Paris.

They once had a labyrinth there. It was inlaid on the cathedral floor at the end of the first third of the nave. The labyrinth was used as a path for meditation, and was popularly known as the "Way to Jerusalem." For those who couldn't afford the grand pilgrimage to Jerusalem it presented itself as a substitute, a sort of pilgrimage in miniature. But clearly people didn't just walk along it in silent reflection; lively, boisterous gangs of children enjoyed it as well. In 1778 a certain Canon Jacquemar had it ripped out—bothered by the cheerful goings-on in the labyrinth. Around the same time labyrinths were likewise removed from other Europeans churches. I wonder why, precisely at the end of the eighteenth century, could grown-ups no longer stand to have children in church? Evidently in the five hundred years preceding, children romping around in the labyrinth hadn't bothered anyone.

In Reims, I fall in love with Gothic architecture. Actually, it's a stone figure that overpowers me, the statue of an angel perched on the west façade. I spend untold minutes gazing into his face and wondering how a stone carving can smile in such a way. The smile seems to emanate not just from the face, but from every atom of its body. I don't know whether I've ever smiled that way in my life. Even now, when I recall that angel, I find myself smiling back. With a soul smiled on by the angel, I enter the cathedral, and am seized by a spontaneous desire to sing here and now, with some great choir of voices.

With my hand I stroke the silent floor stones of Canon Jacquemar. Perhaps some day someone will build the labyrinth back in.

We admire the stained-glass windows—they seem to tell stories that we no longer understand. When I go back outside and turn to say goodbye to my angel, I discover a wall plaque with the inscription "Monument Historique." France has made the labyrinth of Reims the official logo for all its cultural monuments.

Hours later we are standing in front of a different sort of cathedral, a cathedral of death: the charnel house in Verdun. Inside the bones of 130,000 nameless war dead lie in heaps. The whole insanity of war comes crashing into one's consciousness. In the hills of Verdun a giant fortress was built, mainly underground, during the First World War. Year after year the war between the Germans and the French raged over barely shifting battle lines. Who won what here? Nobody knows anymore, except the historians.

What is a gigantic fortress in comparison with a cathedral? How do you compare a cemetery of military dead with an army of exhausted craftsmen? I remember the history class where I learned of the euphoria with which many a soldier marched off to the First World War. Perhaps the glazier who got the order for a cathedral window was seized by a like enthusiasm. Two sorts of zealous men given over body and soul to a cause that demands complete commitment — and one of them stands years later in front of a masterpiece that will bring joy to generations, while the other sinks namelessly into filth and blood. I'm left to wonder if it isn't possible to tell, at the very beginning of a path, whether it will lead to something beautiful or to something catastrophic?

We drive on through a gentle landscape that becomes more and more lovely in the day's dimming light.

The cathedral of Laon is one of the few in northern France that never contained a labyrinth. Nevertheless, when we see it gleaming atop the hill in the twilight, we can't bear to pass it by. Even though we're in the middle of the city, we find a small camping site. The next day we are again taken with the cheerful brightness and quiet beauty of this mighty building and the mild sense of humor with which a stone cow looks down on us from its tower.

3

The Wonder of Gothic

Medieval Christian labyrinth
in the cathedral of Sens, France

*The labyrinth is a sight
for sore eyes,
enlightenment
for the soul,
and a sacred puzzle
for the mind.*

Not all Gothic labyrinths are alike. The basic model, however, seems to be the famous labyrinth at Chartres. It consists of eleven circuits around a large center in the form of a six-petaled rose. In these labyrinths of the Gothic period we see the classical form of the labyrinth undergoing a change. And increasingly, we see the labyrinth being understood as an image of humanity's path through life. The classical labyrinth has seven paths around the center. But to the medieval mind, the number seven is a sacred number, so they thought this would not express the human journey adequately. So, as early as the eighth century, monks began to reconfigure the labyrinth, extending its circuits from seven to eleven. Eleven is a number understood to better suit human beings — because God gave ten commandments, but people always think they know better; and Jesus had twelve apostles, but man always remains imperfect. So the number eleven stands for human excess and imperfection. This Christian understanding also sought to find graphic expression by integrating the cross into the labyrinth. The path of life was to be oriented to this cross and, as it were, supported by the cross. Through a succession of transitioning designs, this reconfiguration was accomplished by the twelfth century. In a number of manuscripts the fully formed "medieval Christian" or "Gothic" labyrinth now makes its appearance.

During construction of the Gothic cathedrals, the labyrinth was built into their floors with variegated plates of marble in such a way that those entering the church are invited to walk through the labyrinth. The path by which one enters the labyrinth at first approaches the center and circles around it several times. Then it leads progressively outward, arching back and forth across the circle with relative regularity. Only when one has reached the final step on the outmost ring does the path turn inward again toward the center.

These labyrinthine paths of reflection, however, are also used in Gothic architecture for an altogether different purpose. As they were in antiquity, they again become a dancing ground. In some ancient church books, we find brief mention of the fact that a traditional Easter dance was to be performed "as usual, in the labyrinth." In some books, however, the dance is described more precisely. In preparation for the dance, they tell us, the youngest priest was to procure a golden yellow ball. After Easter vespers, he handed the ball over to the dean or bishop, while the priests formed a circle around the labyrinth. Then the dean danced the "tripudium," a thumping three-step, through the labyrinth, while the priests danced around the labyrinth in a circle. Throughout the dance the ball, symbolizing the Easter sun rising over the labyrinth, was tossed back and forth between the priests and the dean. After this Easter dance a great banquet was served.

This dance in the church labyrinths was a tradition that lasted for more than three centuries. When I think about our contemporary world, which is surprisingly stiff in so many ways, I like to imagine that deans and bishops might restore this tradition and at least once a year dare to do a little dance with their colleagues. I can readily imagine that such a dance would conjure up a smile on the faces not only of the bishops and priests, but of the entire community and perhaps even the angels.

4

Turnings

Gothic labyrinth in the
cathedral of Amiens, France

*The path to the center
is never straight
but always clear.*

The cathedral of Sens also once had a labyrinth and the tradition of the dance. But the Sens labyrinth varies from the other Gothic labyrinths in some minor details. Not only does its layout contain more half-circles, but its path turns first outward and then slowly and steadily inward. Perhaps this design reveals something of the master architect's understanding of his own path's unfolding toward its center. As in Reims, the Sens cathedral was ripped out, this time in 1768.

The table in our camper invites good conversation. The rain patters away at the camper's thin outer skin, but the smells of gas stove and tea promise comfortable warmth. Traveling light can make the head and heart light. A roof, a cup of hot tea, and a good parking place can be enough to provide us complete satisfaction.

Ulli and I discuss which labyrinthine pattern—the one at Chartres or the one at Sens—corresponds more closely to the paths we follow in pursuit of our real-life goals. Does one feel, at the outset, very near to the goal itself, only to find that the path moves one increasingly away from it? Or is the path rather a constant nearing the center, moving from the outside inward? Our own experiences support both answers.

The path at Chartres reminds us of the course of a love affair. When you first fall in love as a young couple, you find your way toward the center quickly and easily. Then things slowly and steadily move away from the center. That first magnetic pull of love loses its intensity. You perceive yourselves as increasingly distant from your shared center. Some can lose the sense that they travel a shared path at all. But those who choose to go on may find that path returns them again, together, to their common center.

A progressive unbroken nearing of the goal, however, as at Sens, is sometimes the experience one has in a large, creative project. At every step of the work, the feeling grows that one is slowly getting closer and closer to the goal.

In the end, the labyrinth of Chartres strikes us as the more comforting pattern. Just when you've strayed hopelessly far from the goal, it's actually getting closer and closer. You just need to persevere. It's an unfamiliar thought, though one that proves often true:

many who have gotten close have found there's a long way to go, while not all those who have ranged afar are truly far from their goal.

The labyrinth in the cathedral of St. Quentin is built almost exactly like the labyrinth of Chartres. Its center, however, is smaller, and not circular but octagonal. Symbolically, eight is the number of new beginnings. A week has seven days; on the eighth day everything begins anew. The labyrinth is also a path of renewal. Whoever reaches the center and turns around is beginning a brand new path.

The next morning after breakfast our mood of contentment dissolves. We travel north past Paris and reach St. Quentin after three hours on the road. We find the church closed for the lunch break. We return later to find the doors open, and the labyrinth unobstructed by chairs; but a funeral mass has just begun. Still, a Gothic cathedral is vast enough that quiet visitors in the back of the nave won't disturb services. So we make our way over the labyrinth stones, accompanied by organ music and the rites of a requiem mass. Slowly and pensively I put one foot in front of the other. My thoughts turn to Verdun and my own mortality. I turn, and the coffin is thrust into my field of vision; the next turn puts it behind me. The face of the laughing angel comes to mind. His smile contains knowledge that I may never grasp.

I reach the center of the labyrinth, a black octagonal stone. Eight, the number of new beginnings. The liturgy of the resurrection begins. I turn to follow the path back. Everything begins anew; the end of one path is simply the start of a new one.

Amiens lies fifty miles west of St. Quentin, and we try to reach its labyrinth that same day. Like so many others, the Amiens labyrinth was removed in the first years of the nineteenth century, but this one had been reinstalled in 1894. The restored floor plates haven't suffered much wear, and everything still shines in splendid freshness. Unfortunately we can see all this only on a postcard; the church has closed at five, in obedience to its fall schedule. I hesitate—wouldn't it be worth staying one more day to see Amiens? But my curiosity about the English cathedrals gets the upper hand. That night we cross the English Channel.

5

Paths in the Grass

Turf labyrinth in Somerton, England

*More wisdom is to be found
in frequent circling
around the center
than in a quick, one-time success.*

E ngland—land of traditionalists, of strange antiquities, of Stone-henge and ghosts — and the country with the most intact old turf labyrinths. Probably the Gothic church labyrinths of Europe captured the fancies of the English, who brought the idea home for domestication.

Turf labyrinths were laid out in such a way that the grass was cut about eight inches deep in the form of a labyrinth. Some labyrinths were laid out next to the church, others on the grounds of private farms. Still others were laid out on the village green, where the markets were held on a hill nearby. Nine of these labyrinths have been preserved. The first one we're looking for is supposed to be in a little village called Somerton, north of Oxford.

When your travels are guided by a labyrinth book, you get to places where no tourist is likely to have traveled. The only directions we have to go on read: "Outside of Somerton on the property of a private farm, earlier called Troy Town." We circle around narrow, hedge-fringed roads. Fortunately, we know enough English to ask for—and understand—directions from people along the way.

After a while we find the farm. It's somewhat isolated, and, except for a big dog behind the entrance door where we ring, nobody seems to be home. We don't wait long. I try to guess where the labyrinth could be and head off in search of it. After all, with a diameter of fifty feet in close proximity to the farm, it can't be hard to find. Nonetheless it eludes me. But then I find the farmer in an old tool shed. He points me to the other side of the road. There it is, not more than 150 feet from the house.

No one knows why it was built. The farm has changed hands several times. But in recent decades it has been recut roughly every ten years, so that it never disappeared. It's constructed in the classical form, with fifteen circuits. In order to get more than seven circuits you have to insert two or more right angles instead of one.

I make a discovery that will be echoed throughout our journey. I've been assuming that the English were introduced to the idea of the labyrinth in their visits to the Gothic French cathedrals. But now I'm standing in front of a labyrinth that casts doubt on this theory. Why don't we then see a copy of the Gothic form here? Where did the English builder encounter this more ancient classical form? Could the labyrinth perhaps have older roots in England itself? Could it even date there to pre-Christian times?

Little Hannah runs along the lines as if she has been doing it all her life. I know that children like to follow paths, but the labyrinth seems to exercise a special magic. She is so totally absorbed that the whole world around her seems to disappear. At some point her concentration draws me into its spell. My wife too has stopped surveying the surroundings and follows our daughter with her eyes. We watch her for some minutes. I know that if I called to her now, I'd be interrupting something special. The mystery of what is happening here is beyond my understanding. Then around the corner comes the farmer with his barking dog. Hannah looks up mid-stride. She doesn't see the turn ahead and falls into the interstice. The magic dissipates, but we will encounter it again in our adventures with the labyrinth.

The farmer is a newcomer to this property; he doesn't know much about the labyrinth, When he's returned to his work, and I've snapped my pictures, I walk along the labyrinth by myself. Though it looks small, its paths are long. It seems endless, in fact. Its actual length, I later read, is about 365 yards. I can't imagine that this length was deliberately chosen to corresponds to the number of days in the year, but who knows? At least it's a felicitous coincidence. That's life, I think: the paths to the center are indeed long. Standing, at last, in the center of the labyrinth, a tree in the background catches my eye. It's an old giant, already partly dead. Might it have been planted on the day the labyrinth was inaugurated, to stand facing the new arrivals and greet them?

6

In Hedgerows and Deserts

Five-star labyrinth
in the altiplano of Nasca, Peru

*As she walks along, a person learns
to listen to her soul.*

At a tourist information office we hear about a labyrinth museum in Symonds Yat, not far from Ross-on-Wye near Gloucester. Naturally we can't pass that by, and the museum becomes our destination for the next day. At Symonds Yat, a man named Lindsay Heyes has laid out both the labyrinth museum and an accompanying maze. When we arrive, however, the doors are bolted, and a sign reads, "Closed Mondays." Today, as luck would have it, is Monday.

Experienced sojourners that we are, we refused to accept such signs at face value. Our spirits are too high to permit us to settle into disappointment. We're not yet ready to admit defeat. We break out our lunches, stand around, look, and wait. Perhaps something will happen, a new path will open, a new bend in the road will come into view. We're beginning to find ourselves speaking the language of the labyrinth.

After two hours I feel the urge to do something, so I climb over a fence. Calmly and cooly, I enter the maze. I search for the correct path among the hedges, which somehow have a touch of the sinister about them. I worry briefly about getting disoriented, but I don't really believe that will happen. More likely, there will be a gardener behind the next bend, and he'll curse my illegal forced entry. All seems quiet, but you never know what lurks around the next corner in a maze. In the center I find a beautiful marble summerhouse, a hidden, romantic spot, perfect for trysting. I look around a bit more and then take the exit path to the museum's outdoor exhibits. Just then an alarm goes off. How embarrassing. Without panic, but as quickly as possible, I look for the path to the place where I crept in, and jump back over the fence again.

My wife meets me with a look that combines concern, reproach, and a question.

"Yes, that was me," I admit.

We return to our picnicking place. I keep an eye on the still-locked gate. Maybe the owner will come now, summoned by the alarm; maybe he'll make an exception and open the museum to me. But he doesn't come; no one comes. The siren howls for a quarter of an hour. That's rather a long time. When it finally stops, we discuss the next stage of our journey and pack up. It's time to give up our museum visit.

At that moment a bus pulls up and spews out a group of school children. I immediately realize that the turn toward the goal has been accomplished. Lindsay Heyes himself exits the museum and unlocks the gates. We immediately launch into an animated conversation. He says that he's been meaning to get around to adjusting the alarm differently so that it won't be tripped by every cat in the neighborhood. I nod and don't give myself away. Then he guides me through his museum; as we walk, he tells me the story of his remarkable discovery that one of the famous figures at Nasca is actually a labyrinth.

Nasca is a magic word to those fascinated by archaeological puzzles. The high plain of Peru harbors one of the greatest mysteries of human history. Sketched onto the landscape there are giant figures: a spider, a monkey, a hummingbird, a lizard, a condor, and more. These figures are discernable only from the air, as each measures between one hundred and five hundred yards long. Interspersed with these animal and bird figures are lines which often stretch for miles through the countryside, and other still unexplained geometric drawings. Over the centuries Indian tribes living on this plain produced these figures by sweeping away the top layer of the soil, which consists of dark pebbles, exposing the bright-colored sand that lies beneath. Why they did this has yet to be determined.

One of the forms at Nasca resembles a sort of flower.

"It's a labyrinth," says Heyes, "built according to the same principle as the classical one. The classical labyrinth is drawn from an intersection, four corners and four points. Just now I'm drawing one from a five-star and five points."

I am astonished how simple this is; yet until Heyes's discovery none of the scholars studying Nasca had noticed it.

Lindsay shows me the treasures of his collection: drawings of hedge labyrinths, design rules, and photos from all over the world. Then he launches into a complicated explanation of why the symbol of the labyrinth was never used in China. My thoughts remain behind in Nasca. If its flower is indeed a labyrinth, then was it a path meant to be walked? Was it perhaps a processional path or a dancing ground? Perhaps the other figures too were built as paths for processions. I have to take a closer look at this. I urgently need a book about Nasca.

The schoolchildren rouse me from my reverie. They're playing tag in the maze. I stand on a platform and observe the merry goings-on. They scream and laugh. Thank God the creature coming around the corner is the boy who's "it" — and not the Minotaur.

As we drive on, my thoughts turn back to Peru.

"How did the labyrinth get to Nasca?"

"They must have discovered it," Ulli suggests.

It's the only known five-star labyrinth in the world. What is its genesis? I count myself among those excited by the possibilities that another theory presents. From my labyrinth guide book I've learned that some North American Indian tribes were familiar with the labyrinth. And I can easily imagine that there were travelers — then as now — who were eager to venture far and wide. Perhaps a North American Indian traveled south to Peru and showed tribes there how to build a labyrinth. Could the five-pointed star be their own original variation on a known theme?

Yet I'm still afraid that Ulli has the final say when she notes: "We'll probably never know."

Still, we're left with the incredible thought that at Nasca the largest ancient labyrinth in the world was carved out of the soil.

Our next destination is a tiny, dreamy spot in the middle of England. At the center of the turf labyrinth of Hilton there is a white pillar. On it I read that the labyrinth was installed in 1660 by a nineteen-year-old named William Sparrow. Back in Somerton we had assumed that in a turf labyrinth one walks down in the trenches; but now we discover that as a rule people walk on the raised turf that has remained. We run along these raised paths and enjoy the pleasant, peaceful atmosphere. The site has been well chosen: it is palpably a place of power. The white pillar ends in a ball. I follow my urge to shinny up and hoist myself on top of it. After I've balanced myself, I stretch my arms upward. "Axis mundi," the center of the world, I can't help thinking.

7

It's a Long Way

Labyrinth in the cathedral of Ely

*The direct path to a goal
may be short and straight;
but nothing worthwhile
can be reached simply or quickly.*

The English cathedrals are impressive in their own right. We visit one in Ely, near Cambridge. Founded in 673 as a monastery, the building of the church proper began in 1083. English Gothic is different from the French; it's much more colorful and playful. Directly beyond the entrance door in the Ely atrium lies a labyrinth, inserted into the floor pattern. I'm already a step into it before I notice it. It was a very late addition, built in 1870, and you can tell. Though decorative, it somehow doesn't fit in. Its paths are hard to negotiate; the turns are narrow and sharp, a challenge to the whole body. The path to the center is about two hundred feet long; when you reach it and look up, you see looming two hundred feet overhead an image of Christ the Pantocrator painted on the ceiling. Anyone who gets to the center has ipso facto come upon the face of God.

Beside the path into the labyrinth is a modern statue of Christ, which depicts him as a brother by the side of the road, a wounded healer. As fine a symbolic touch as this is, the Ely atrium strikes me as cold, and the labyrinth itself as devoid of power. In my previous labyrinth walks there has always been a tension, which I have found moving: between the long paths and the surprising turns, between my joy at being on the way and my growing impatience, between the apparently meaningless details and the power of the completed whole.

One senses little of that tension in Ely. What a frightful feeling it must be to have life pull you around in such sharp turns and narrow pathways, I think. Even the idea that Christ stands by your path, awaiting your exit, can't quite banish that feeling.

I leave the atrium behind me and enter a church that plays with light the way Bach plays with the organ. Here it is again, the wonder of the Gothic, the smile of the angel.

We leave Ely and drive past Cambridge, heading south toward Saffron Walden. The Brits are glad to give precise directions, so that we have no trouble finding the largest turf labyrinth still in existence. Two boys are playing soccer on it, and I debate whether or not to ask them to stand aside so I can take pictures. But children's play seems to me somehow part and parcel of labyrinths, so I say nothing. No one knows when this labyrinth was created; the first mention of it in historical literature is in 1699. At its widest point it has a diameter of 140 feet; it's constructed with fifteen circuits. The path is arched out at the four corners, as with the labyrinth of the cathedral at Reims. A tree once stood in its center, but it was destroyed by lightning on November 5, 1823.

I hesitate. I know what an undertaking it would be to go into this labyrinth. A classical labyrinth has seven turns; the Gothic variety has twenty-eight; but Saffron Walden was seventy-four. The path in St. Quentin is 750 feet long, the one in Somerton 1,100 feet, but Saffron Walden is over 4,800 feet. I know that the paths through the labyrinths of my life are long as well. Don't be frightened by the turnings along the way; just go on—you'll get there. That's the great wisdom, the hope that is the gift of the labyrinth. Yet in the end, I don't walk the labyrinth because its length scares me. I look at my watch and I choose to move on to something new. That's how it often is with me in life. I saw the Saffron Walden labyrinth, but because I did not walk it, to this day I don't really know it.

There is a little old turf labyrinth in Wing near Uppingdale. We meet a family with whom we're friendly and drive there together. We find the labyrinth hidden alongside a path, surrounded by a white wooden fence. It lies there with no recognizable connection to its surroundings. The first thing our friends say is:

"What, that's all?"

My enthusiastic descriptions have evidently given them a different impression of what a labyrinth will be like. Somewhat uncertain we all stand at the white wooden fence, when the labyrinth begins to reveal its power. The three children run in, the bigger ones first, with Hannah, the smallest, behind them. The paths are worn down in some places, and the route can't always be clearly detected. When Hannah loses her way, the others come back to help. The same thing happens again; but soon all three children are sitting happily in the center and hugging each other. And the whole process begins all over again; I stop counting how many times they run the labyrinth. At some point my daughter clasps my pant leg in exhaustion.

"Now I'm going to go, too," I say.

"Hannah's coming," she says.

That evening in the pub my friends reflect, "At first, we were disappointed. But there really is something special about the labyrinth."

8

What You Learn
with Your Feet

2	2	4	1	3
3	3	1	3	2
1	2	○	2	3
3	2	3	2	4
4	2	1	3	2

⇧

Modern numerical labyrinth

If you haven't grasped it with your hands,
you can't comprehend it.
If you don't go there with your feet,
you can't understand it.

"**A**re we really in England?" my wife asks me the next morning, looking up at the sky. Another cloudless day is in the offing. Since we crossed the Channel fourteen days ago, we haven't seen a drop of rain. It will stay that way for another week. Even November can be a good time for traveling.

We ramble on toward St. Albans, home of the best-known labyrinth architect of our time. Armed with a bad map, we hunt for a camping place. More often than not we get lost. One traffic circle has four, another six, exits. We take one after the other till we hit on the right one. Life may be a labyrinth, but traffic is a maze. Wrong decisions are just lost time. Or maybe every false decision is ultimately necessary for finding the right one. There's not much time for philosophizing, though, because just then the engine breaks down.

The car is in the repair shop, the camper parked on a narrow side street; but the labyrinth builder, Adrian Fisher, lives only a short walk away. Soon I'm sitting across from him in his jam-packed study. With the usual enthusiasm of the expert he tells me about labyrinths, his own and others. I am particularly fascinated by his schoolyard mazes.

"What's behind them," he explains, "is the principle of the labyrinth: namely, to acquire wisdom with joy and curiosity. The labyrinth teaches you without your noticing."

He asks me whether I want to see how they work; and we lay out two labyrinths together in the garden. One of them is a numerical labyrinth. A square is divided into twenty-five little boxes; all except the center box are inscribed with a number between one and four. To add to the challenge each number is also marked as a positive or negative number. The objective is to reach the center marked "zero," in a specified number of steps, in such a way that the sum of all the numbered squares stepped on equals zero as well. I place myself on the starting square. It has the number one, so I can take one step. You can step vertically or horizontally. I step aside and find myself on number three, so I can take three steps. Now I have to try to find my way through the labyrinth, as I keep moving the prescribed number of steps ahead. Then at some point I reach the center, with exactly the right number of steps.

"I hope you're not a math teacher," Adrian says, as I keep making mistakes when I add or subtract. I feel a surge of ambition. Had I been able to study arithmetic this way, I would have done it enthusiastically for hours. I wouldn't be so embarrassingly dependent today on a pocket calculator. Adrian laughs. "If you had learned arithmetic with your feet, you could do it better." I know. There are lots of things that you learn better with your feet than with your head. We go on to play another schoolyard maze, the "arrow labyrinth." Through these games, I experience the fascinating power of the labyrinth in a whole new way.

When the car is drivable again, I pay a visit to yet another labyrinth specialist. Jeff Saward owns the world's largest archive on the subject of labyrinths; it's a secret research station. Here I get answers to the questions that have piled up thus far.

"How did the labyrinth come to Nasca?" is the first question I put to him.

"Well, Nasca is an anomaly. Even though we find two labyrinths there, they're the only labyrinths in all of South America. That's what makes it so hard. We know more about how the labyrinth came to North America, although here too there are many puzzles. The labyrinth was surely in North America before the Europeans came. What we find there is still the pure classical form, though it's varied in little distinctive features of the design. It appears as petroglyphs, on clay tablets, saddle covers, and silver jewelry; and we've found it once or twice laid out with stones on the floor. But the labyrinth is found only in very limited regions of North America: among the Hopi, Navajo, Pima, and Papago Indians. Their origin stories tell of how they came from over the ocean, and they use the labyrinth as a sign of entrance into the new world. So it's a sign of their new birth."

"You mean that the Hopis were seafarers, who already knew the labyrinth from the Mediterranean Basin?"

"You see, we find the same labyrinth in Crete, Afghanistan, Pakistan, India, Sri Lanka, Indonesia, and then on the west coast of America. You can't exclude the possibility that groups of immigrants didn't cross the Pacific to America until late, and that they were already familiar with old symbols from Europe. Perhaps we simply underestimate the ability of ancient peoples to have traveled. The labyrinths in the Mediterranean Basin, India, and the Americas are amazingly similar; in the strict sense, they're practically identical."

Then he tells me the strange story of a petroglyph researcher who claimed to have found fifty old Indian labyrinths in the American Southwest and Mexico. He pulls out a sheaf of photocopies from one of his many files.

"These are from books by Carl Schuster. They're rare, because they were only privately printed. The material in them is truly unique as Carl Schuster was a scholar after his own style. He lived in 1902 till 1967 and collected tribal symbols from all over the world. His idée fixe was that somehow everything fit together. He compared cultures that were geographically far removed from each other, always looking for the link, the commonality between them. His efforts went counter to the prevailing opinions of the cultural anthropologists of his day, who believed that each culture had to be viewed in isolation. It seemed completely absurd to them to compare Masai with Eskimos, or Greeks with Indians. Schuster was an academic outsider: he published almost nothing and was never invited to lectures or conferences. Instead, he spent his time out and about collecting. Then he died; and thousands of boxes, filled with more than 30,000 photos, travel reports, and sketches, were just left lying around. No one would have taken any interest in them, were it not for a man named Ed Carpenter. He heard about this remarkable archive and decided to publish as much of it as possible. No publishing house would take it; but once Carpenter had the financial means to do so he published Schuster's collection himself, in a fascinating twelve-volume set. One of these volumes addresses labyrinths, and it includes some things that only Schuster knew. There are only a few copies of these books in existence; virtually no libraries have them. But they are in the

Ethnology Museum in Basel. Incidentally, Schuster's whole original archive is stored there. It took an entire room to house the collection."

I spontaneously envisage a cluttered room, full of yellowed pages, boxes, and dust-covered treasures. Of course, I know the image is inspired by the Indiana Jones movies, but I decide on the spot that I must visit that room.

"By the way, it could have been the Normans, too."

I had slipped off into the world of secret rooms, and was only listening with half an ear.

"What about the Normans?"

"Well, the stone labyrinths laid out in Mexico match the ones in Scandinavia. In Scandinavia today you can find more than three hundred old stone labyrinths, mainly on the coasts. I'm fairly certain that the Normans were introduced to the labyrinth during their journeys and raids on Italy and integrated it into their own culture. And we know that the Normans were also in America."

"Yes, but it's a long way from Newfoundland to Mexico."

"Sure, but how often do we think that we know it all, until the facts turn out to be quite different? Personally, I think it's most likely the labyrinth came across the Pacific. Oh, and the Normans also built a stone labyrinth in England. It's in the Isles of Scilly off the coast of Cornwall. There were probably more stone labyrinths here in England long ago, but this is the only one we know of. In Germany, it was the Scandinavians, too."

"In Germany?"

"Yes, there are three turf labyrinths that have been preserved in Germany. One of them is popularly called the Sweden Ring, because Swedish soldiers supposedly built it during the Thirty Years War. Earlier there may have been something like a hundred turf labyrinths in Germany. We have detailed information about thirty or so of them."

Jeff gives me documentation on these labyrinths and how to find them. He's still shaking his head over how long it took him to find one of them, the labyrinth in the Eilenrieder Forest in Hanover. Even when he was a mere fifty yards away from it, none of the people walking by had any idea that an old labyrinth was there.

That evening, my mind is full of images. I see dancing Indians with labyrinths painted on their chests; Vikings gathering stones on a foggy coast; children, lit by a full moon, meeting secretly at a lawn labyrinth on a hill near their village; and a proud young chief standing on the wild plains of Nasca, holding a piece of leather on which is sketched the blueprint of a classical labyrinth. He is saying:

"No, let's not use that one. I just got a different idea."

9

Map of the Soul

Modern flagstone labyrinth
in Grey's Court, England

The labyrinth
inimitably reflects
the path of humanity
through time,
It lures the human race to the center —
into the here and now.

The path to Grey's Court, twenty miles west of the city limits of London, is a hedge-lined maze. Little English country roads are always swathed in shrubbery. With a camper in tow, the quest to find some tiny village in the "backwoods" of England can be nerve-wracking. Over the last stretch of road we've followed an amiable Englishman—the third person to tell us that Grey's Court closed long ago. But seeing for ourselves has proved a good strategy so far. And sure enough, when we get there, we discover that while the castle is closed, the labyrinth lies accessible, outside the garden walls. It was built by Adrian Fisher in 1981. He doesn't agree with me, but I think it's his masterpiece. Never before or since have I walked through a labyrinth where my inner and outer self vibrated in such harmony. Of course, many factors come together to create such an experience, and on this day everything seems to be in synch. Going through this labyrinth is wonderful, a nearly perfect exercise in mediation. My walk is relaxed, and I soon slip into a light-hearted, radiant state. It is a blissful, contented inward listening. My soul seems to be saying to me: Hello, it's so nice to see you.

Since that day I've been convinced that in building labyrinths there must be a holy rule similar to the golden section. In Grey's Court it was realized, either deliberately or by mere guesswork. The center is encircled by seven large-scale arcs; all the curves are soft and sweeping. The rhythm of the movement is completely in tune with my inner self, as if it were the map of my soul, spread out on the ground.

In the center I find there's a stone block with the following inscription:

> Credo, says the heart,
> Upheld in cradling hands.
> The heart has reasons
> No reason understands.
> Mind's flashing messages
> Fork and fall apart.
> At the center stillness.
> Credo, says the heart.

The walk alone has so moved me, and now—these words. I quickly call to Ulli and show her the poem. Unfortunately, I haven't managed to trust my feelings. Had I given them free rein, I might have fallen to my knees and wept. Instead I call to someone to tell of my discovery, to secure it in explanation. It seems my way to conceal my open soul behind the cloak of words.

Now I also discover an iron globe mounted on the stone block; into it is fixed a sundial. In the center, I think to myself, the human person is also fixed in space and time. I'm finally all there, my being has arrived in the Here and Now, and my heart is secure in faith. It's too bad this gift was more than I could stand.

I know that I can't go through the labyrinth a second time, secretly hoping that it will touch me again in the same way. When you expect the extraordinary to happen, it never does. It can only come unexpectedly, as a gift. Maybe I'll get another chance somewhere else.

10

The First Step

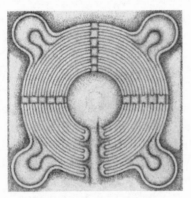

The largest preserved turf labyrinth,
in Saffron Walden, England

On a path two great crises await you.
The first comes when the magic of the beginning has vanished.
The second comes just before the goal.
Both ask the question:
Do you really want this?

In the Bath city park, Adrian Fisher has built yet another labyrinth of flagstones. Hannah and Ulli quickly run through it to the center. I concentrate first on taking my photos. I climb up walls, ponder whether this or that tree would provide a good perspective for viewing the whole site. At the center of the labyrinth is a domed mosaic. I am curious what's to be seen on it. To charge straight through, though, simply head for the center, will take some overcoming of myself. It's as if I were contemplating the violation of a holy space, an unspoken rule: You can only go to the center if you're also taking the whole journey. To simply go heedlessly through it would be barbaric. But really, it's a new sort of labyrinth, I tell myself. It was built entirely for the commercial purposes of an exposition. It serves merely as a source of fun. The excuses I give myself, though, don't work. I stand in the center and photograph the mosaic, feeling like a tourist who's entered a church in Italy wearing a bathing suit. Then I store my equipment and sit down on a bench.

You can just begin again, I tell myself, and place myself at the entrance to the labyrinth.

"Come on, we've been here long enough. Let's go back to town; we're hungry." My wife presses me. I stand in front of the first flagstone and think: the first step, that's the most important decision. The first step contains the whole path. With the first step I tie an invisible thread to the goal. This thread is the guideline for everything that follows. Even if the goal appears indistinct or, in some cases, entirely redefined until you're under way, with the first step the connection is made.

I look toward the center. I feel that I've dishonored it once already; but now I'm ready to try again. I don't know where this particular path will lead, how much patience it will demand, or how many questions and crises await me. But I'm ready to seek the center afresh, to let the path guide me to it this time.

A small voice pulls me down from my stratospheric intellectual flight.

"Daddy, I'm hungry."

In this labyrinth too the path will remain untaken.

Later Ulli and I chat about the power that lies in the first step. The first step of a project, an idea, or a play usually sets in motion a surprising dynamic. Doors open, kindred spirits report for duty, help comes from some critical quarter. Sometimes it seems as if the whole universe has been waiting for this step to be taken; and I'm amazed that I've never noticed it waiting there before.

In every first step lies a special feeling, the magic of the beginning. This magic is a splendid wind beneath your wings. It carries you almost effortlessly to the first great crisis of your journey, when the magic disappears. On most paths, crisis visits a second time. The first comes after just starting out, and the last just before the goal. It's as if you were being asked the same question twice: Do you really want this? Is this the path you want to take? Is this the goal you really want to reach? The first crisis takes the wind out of your sails, the spring out of your step. Anyone who now finds the "yes" to go on still has a long way ahead. The labyrinth is the symbol of the path that everyone who tackles a serious matter must travel on.

11

The Monster in the Mirror

Labyrinth center made up of eight linked mirrors,
in a sketch by Leonardo da Vinci

*If life is viewed as a maze,
every mistake is an unnecessary detour
and a waste of time.
If life is a labyrinth,
then every mistake is a part of the path
and an indispensable master teacher.*

There is in Bristol a little Gothic church known as Mary Redcliff. Each of the keystones in the Gothic arches of the dome is decorated with a precious stone. All the labyrinths that we've found so far were built for feet. I am surprised to find that there are also labyrinths that shine down from above. I instinctively wish I had a ladder to get closer to the stones, to be able to travel through the labyrinth with my fingers. But the only way to traverse the path of this labyrinth is in a concentrated visual exercise. To travel this distance by eye through a Gothic labyrinth with eleven circuits and twenty-eight turns is strenuous. But it can be done. I think in contrast, of the "Bristol Watermaze," a labyrinth-spring constructed in Bristol's Victoria Park. I consider it a complete failure, because it simply can't be negotiated. Only the water can freely flow along the path of this labyrinth. It takes a while before we realize that you can't do anything with this labyrinth; it's only there to be looked at. The water-filled path is too narrow for your feet, even when a warm summer day would make a cool splash welcome.

Early the next day we leave Bristol and stop in Wookey Hole. There we find a charming combination of attractions: a colorful historical museum; the Mirror Maze, a sort of old-fashioned Hall of Mirrors; and a series of underground caves. We learn a bit of history that disturbs me: in the eighteen century a pair of bored soldiers shot out a splendid hall of stalactites in the cave. One stalactite after another was "cleared away." An hour of shooting destroyed a wonder that nature took a thousand years to create. My anger at those idiots won't go away.

"This is the Minotaur," reads the engraving above one of the mirrors we encounter in the mirror maze. I gaze into my own eyes. I can't help but think of the saying, "He who refuses to see the evil in himself will project it onto another." Am I my own monster? I make a face at the mirror. The very first sentence in the labyrinth book, my sole guide on this journey, declares: "In the labyrinth one doesn't meet the Minotaur; one meets oneself." I too belong to the great family of idiots.

12

Mother Earth

The Tor of Glastonbury, England
(Nowadays only the church tower is standing.)

*The labyrinth is a
symbol of the earth,
the womb of the soul,
and a dancing ground.*

From the moment we see the Tor of Glastonbury on the horizon, the place draws us like a magnet. We park on the upper rise of the hill and climb the path to the tower ruins of the former abbey. Strange spirals ring the hill in terraces; what could they be? Are they old processional paths? This is one of England's many mysterious sites. Glastonbury is the mythical Avalon, the island on which King Arthur died, and where his queen, Guinevere, was laid to rest.

One of the most impressive abbeys in the world had been built at the base of this hill in the twelfth century. Its library contained a wealth of treasures, both of its own time and from antiquity. The abbey was built atop the site of the first stone church erected in England. There are claims that even earlier — as early as 64 A.D. — Glastonbury was also the site of the first Christian community in England, founded by Joseph of Arimathea, the great-uncle of Jesus who gave his tomb for Jesus' interment after the Crucifixion. During the twelfth-century construction of the new church, the coffins of King Arthur and Guinevere were found in the monastic cemetery, and their remains were later moved to a marble tomb in front of the new abbey's high altar.

We stand in the evening light amid the sparse remains of the great abbey's walls. A small white plastic sign marks the site of the former grave of King Arthur. In 1539, an abbot of Glastonbury who had the effrontery to criticize the divorce of Henry VIII was hanged on Glastonbury Tor. That same year when the king dissolved monasteries across the land, the abbey was sold and demolished.

Who is this Minotaur, the monster in the labyrinth of our soul? How is it possible that human beings can destroy such works of greatness? Is there no spark of reverence for age and beauty?

In Glastonbury's mysterious shops, redolent of aromatic oils, you can find practically anything on the subject of mysticism and esoteric goods. We go off in search of labyrinth jewelry. Though this particular Glastonbury quest proves fruitless, I do enjoy another strange experience. We meet a group of "Tribal People," modern gypsies who are seeking a more authentic life, rooted in nature. We speak at length with them about God and the Goddess; Mother Earth, Moon, and Sun; about fire rituals; and Samhain, the last day in the Celtic year—celebrated this very day. It isn't hard to understand the attraction of turning the mind back to our earthly roots of being. Too much has been destroyed by Christianity and the Enlightenment; too much as been sacrificed to rationality. All too often God has been presented as a harsh and joyless father, subjugator of a creation that he doesn't love.

"The labyrinth is the belly of the mother," one man says; "the umbilical cord leading to the earth."

"It's the dance of the women," says a woman, "and you men will never understand it."

13

No Time for the Path

Labyrinth on Winchester Hill, England

*Those who travel along too quickly
often hurry past the center
without noticing it.*

The last English labyrinth that we want to visit lies on a hill near Winchester. We park at the great cathedral and duck inside it first. Again we are impressed by the monumental size and lively interior that are hallmarks of the Gothic. A priest is checking to see how the colors of a festive new cassock look against the backdrop of the altar cloth, his colleagues and a group of determined women offering their commentaries; the priest sighs. His cassock resembles a woman's dress. I catch myself thinking: These priest have a hard time, always forced to replace the lost mother in the Church.

It's a long and beautiful walk to Cathrine's Hill, though the heavy rains have drenched the ground. Walking past buildings and embankments, we approach the hill, which wears a circle of trees like a crown. All at once two barking dogs charge toward us, no owner in sight. I quickly lift Hannah to my shoulders. They rush away as fast as they came, but they leave behind an unpleasant tension in the air.

The labyrinth lies in front of the trees. Its dramatic location overlooking the city makes it unique among turf labyrinths. Here history still breathes, even if constricted by the city streets and building projects below. When the labyrinth was laid out four hundred years ago, a chapel stood beneath the trees. Now only a few stones remain. How much this place has witnessed beneath these tall, slender trees! Speeding cars now whir past at its feet. Pilgrims here have become rare; we feel that we are strange creatures, indeed, to have come to this place to walk unhurriedly along its primordial lines. The wind has heaped autumn leaves in the hollows of the paths, giving a wonderful coloration to the whole labyrinth, with contrasting browns and greens. It spurs me to wonder, how many people have taken this path before me? If only one person walked it each day since its creation, that would make 130,000 of us.

In the department store in Crawley a labyrinth game has been laid out on the floor. We are in the neighborhood, so we stop there. Masses of people are out doing their Saturday shopping, but none of them pay any attention to the pattern under their feet. Only when Ulli and I walk a few rounds do others stop and discover in amazement that the mosaic on the floor is what's causing our laughter. After a while we infect a few of them with our pleasure. The game is still going on when we head off to do some shopping of our own. But when we return, the flow of men and women who ignore the floor beneath their feet dominates the place one again.

Slowly our circle tour through southern England winds down. Before we reach the coast to recross the Channel, we make one last stop in the small town of Leeds, southeast of London.

The hedge labyrinth was built at incredible cost in Leeds Castle. It's a difficult one to negotiate, with a little hill to be reached in the center. From there a path leads down into the depths, opening into a beautiful underground grotto. A gigantic statue in the grotto fountain has water flowing from its mouth; everything is decorated with bizarre shells. It's exciting in its slightly eerie beauty.

"What is your greatest fear?" I ask Ulli that evening. "To get truly lost," she says. I sense what she means and ask no more questions.

That evening I get sick. I have no idea what I've caught; it brings strange symptoms and complete exhaustion. The flickering images in my head get more and more bewildering; fever is the maze of the mind. I thank God for leaving a backdoor in this maze—sleep.

14

The Pearl

Labyrinth in the Cologne cathedral

You're in the center,
and no path to you
is too long.

U lli drives through the night. Not until we get to the German border does my consciousness slowly find its way back into the labyrinth of life.

Around eight in the evening we reach the city limits of Cologne. As we near the city center, we feel a touch of despair. With so many parking places reserved for residents, driveways, and the like, it's impossible to find a place for the camper that's neither creepily isolated nor right out on a main street. We can't decide which direction to take. But suddenly a spot materializes near a high-rise, away from the street but still well lit. Nearby is a subway stop, a pharmacy, and the shingle of a general practitioner. It's unbelievable, and yet perfectly to be expected. Why is it so hard for us to grow to trust in a good path?

In Germany there was supposedly only one old church labyrinth, namely St. Severin's in Cologne. No one knows what it used to look like or how it got lost. But a new labyrinth has appeared in modern Cologne. It was built in 1977, to celebrate the completion of the construction of the Cologne cathedral. Many people have taken issue with building a labyrinth inside a Christian church, but I disagree. The labyrinth is, among other things, a symbol of the Resurrection. Anyone who is carried down into the symbolic crypt that the center of the labyrinth represents has completed his or her life's path. The sojourner has arrived at the goal, the center. But one doesn't remain trapped here: in the resurrection, the path to new life will be opened up. Ariadne's thread leads Theseus to love; the imprisoned Greek hostages are led out of the labyrinth and returned to their lives. Just so, there is a divine thread of love that will lead all prisoners out of the labyrinths of their lives.

The labyrinth in the Cologne cathedral is too small to walk. It's one of those maddening labyrinths that neither look like what you had imagined nor are in the place where they are expected to be. Many assert that the placement of the labyrinth at the stairway down to the crypt is the wrong place for a labyrinth within a church, but I disagree.

~

We hear that another church labyrinth exists somewhere in Germany. First the name Würzburg pops up, then Ellwangen. We make a few more inquiries, and finally we seem to be on the right track. In Hohenberg near Ellwangen, in the church of St. James, there is a newly installed labyrinth.

The church rectory is one of a kind. The pastor, Sieger Köder, is an artist who has painted its interior. He has also decorated the interior of the parish church, becoming something of a local celebrity in the process. He has had a small octagonal labyrinth laid out in flagstone in front of the altar. The centerpiece is especially beautiful: a bronze mussel with a pearl. In one of the Gospel parables, Jesus presents the model of the merchant who gives everything he has for a precious pearl. That's how it should also be with the Kingdom of God. What's really precious to us should be worth everything we have and are. Such a radical "everything," though, is incredibly hard to risk. What if it turns out that you've deceived yourself, after betting everything on one card? Then you've lost everything.

~

I often block myself from taking risks by opening up too many possibilities. There's Plan A or Plan B, perhaps even Plan C. Yet it's obvious that until I commit to a particular path, I'll stay stuck where I am. I can't take a single step so long as I'm afraid to turn my back on every other possibility. When my energies move only toward keeping my escape routes open, then I actually go nowhere.

God listens to prayers, but he also has an army of helpers (humans, angels, vicissitudes, and crises) who have a holy respect for human freedom. As long as I refuse to make a choice, they'll set nothing in motion; they won't intervene prematurely. Their help comes to those who have committed themselves without reservation. The pearl can be won only by one who stakes it all on a single card.

15

Paths of Pilgrimage

Turf labyrinth in Boughton Green, England

*After a while I know neither
how far I have to go,
nor how far I've gone.
I begin to concentrate on the path,
not on the distance.*

In a brochure about the church of St. James Hohenberg, I find a reference to the Path of St. James. It's an old pilgrims' road leading through Europe to Santiago de Compostela in Spain. This is the first I've heard of it. The labyrinth and the Path of St. James, both paths of pilgrimage; the connection rouses my curiosity.

The autumn is drawing to a close, and we head to our winter quarters in Innsbruck. I want to learn more about the Path of St. James, and what the labyrinth might have to do with it. I'm glad that there's room in our camper for a small research library.

For thousands of years people have set out on pilgrimage. Even today, the journey to Mecca for Muslims or to the Ganges for Hindus counts as one of the prescribed duties of human life. Christendom too has its tradition of pilgrimage. Since the beginning of Christianity Jerusalem and Rome have been considered the great goals; more recently other sites made sacred by holy apparitions or miracles have been added, such as Lourdes and Fatima.

But the pilgrimage to Santiago de Compostela in far western Spain seems to be something quite special. The coffin of James the Elder, one of Jesus' twelve Apostles, is said to have miraculously appeared here for burial from over the sea. But it's not tribute to this particular apostle that has made this route the most traveled pilgrimage in the Christian world. It's the path itself: a path to the West, toward the setting sun, to the farthest tip of the continent, the *finis terrae,* the end of the world.

This path of pilgrimage had such importance during the Middle Ages that everywhere along the European pilgrim's path one comes upon places of tribute—churches of St. James, customs of St. James, and inns of St. James.

We pass the winter in Innsbruck, a city whose cathedral is likewise dedicated to St. James the Elder. Innsbruck historically has enjoyed a strategic location on the greatest transit route in Europe; a stream of traders and pilgrims has always flowed through this city. I read one day in the newspaper that the square in front of the cathedral is going to be reconstructed. I immediately think: a labyrinth should be built there—a St. James labyrinth, a miniature path of pilgrimage to imitate the great one. And just as spontaneously I begin to plan my first labyrinth. I want to try something new, without losing any of the powerful symbolism contained in the old forms. I doodle a little and suddenly discover something like a figure in the lower half of my labyrinth sketch. That has to stay. I work it out more clearly until I can plainly recognize it—the dancing James. Now I orient the path to the cross, moving first toward the center and then outward. After a few trials, it's obvious that I can't have everything. To bring in something new is to give something else up. But I'm content with my dancing James. I'm convinced that my sketch is a perfectly coherent layout for a labyrinth in front of a pilgrimage church.

So far no one else knows about my idea, but in my private enthusiasm I collect all the information I'd need to carry it out. I get a stonemason to estimate the cost of cutting out various colored flagstones. It's no small amount, but the labyrinth has quickly captured the interest of the stonemason, too, and he works out the most efficient technical solution to the problems of its creation. Without intending to he takes my plan one step further, and inadvertently makes a special contribution to the symbolism.

"We have the gray granite here," he says, "but I'd have to order the green from Spain." Then the very floor of the labyrinth itself would be tied to the goal of the pilgrims' longing.

Taking my plans and cost estimate, I go to the city councilor in charge of the cathedral square reconstruction project. I'm so enthusiastic about my idea that I'm sure I can win him over to the cause immediately. We can begin building next month! But I forget that worthwhile path takes a labyrinthine course.

Time passes. The cathedral square has been rebuilt, provisionally, without a labyrinth. The layout idea has been passed around to the city authorities. It was pronounced good and then rejected; reconsidered, and dropped again. Many twists and turns have been taken, but in this story the center has yet to be reached.

16

Just at the Point of Giving Up

Floor labyrinth in the church of
San Vitale in Ravenna, Italy

*Anyone without a dream to lose
has already lost everything.*

Traveling again, now on our way south, we are playing Italian music and feeling more free and easy than we had in England or the North. Spring has just arrived; there's still plenty of snow on the mountains, which slowly recede behind us. In Mantua we turn off the highway and park near the city wall. In the old part of the city is a large piazza, dotted with café chairs and umbrellas. From the postcard stand in front of the kiosk I can see the gold-blue labyrinth ceiling in the Palazzo Ducale, shining toward me.

The Mantuan princely family of the Gonzagas loved the labyrinth. It appears to have held a sustained interest for them; it's found both in pieces of art that they commissioned and in decorative additions to their houses. In their enormous Palazzo Ducale, there is a *sala de labirinti,* a hall of labyrinths — unfortunately closed, no admission. "Prego," I stammer, "please, specialistico labirinto austriaco, foto, prego, uno minuti." Almost all Italian museum guards have some understanding of this sort of thing. Minutes later I lie alone and undisturbed on the floor of the labyrinth room, looking up at the ceiling. Inscribed along the path of the labyrinth are the words: *forse che sí, forse che no* — maybe yes, maybe no. Perhaps for the princes the labyrinth symbolized the weighing of issues; they might have wandered in the labyrinth meditatively, asking for wise counsel. It's a splendid room, an impressive ceiling design. I wonder whether a prince ever lay on the floor as I did, observing the work with such fascination. I hurry with my photos; I don't want to lest the limits of the guard's amiability. I find another room where part of a mural can be seen. It's Mount Olympus, surrounded by a lake in which there is a labyrinth through which a fleet of ships must sail before they can arrive at the mountain. I think of Troy, with its strong connections to the labyrinth and the labyrinthine homecoming of Odysseus. Everyone is an Odysseus; everyone is in the process of traveling through his or her labyrinth, in search of home.

Another interesting Mantuan site is the Sala di Psiche, or Hall of Psyche, in the Palazzo Te. The floor is laid out in eight octagonal labyrinths, which correspond to eight octagonal images on the ceiling. I walk through the room and note the fascinating mosaic technique that forms the center of each labyrinth. From a certain angle you notice a small spring at the center of each labyrinth. It gives the appearance that upon arriving you're offered fresh water. The picture pleases me so much that despite a dubious look from the museum guard I dip a finger in the "spring" and pretend to be drinking from its water.

We travel toward the sea in hopes of finding a comfortable camping place, but it's too early in the season — beginning of April — and all the campgrounds are still closed. I'm impatient to see the labyrinth in Ravenna, at the Basilica of San Vitale. I take no satisfaction in seeing Sant' Apollinare and the other splendid buildings that lie along the way. Will we get to see the labyrinth? How big is it? Will I be able to photograph it from the balustrade above? Will there be benches or mobs of tourists obscuring my view?

San Vitale is a church filled with marvelously beautiful sixth-century mosaics. Thousands of tourists are guided through it in the high season; and now we happen to have arrived on a feast day. The labyrinth lies in front of us, hardly noticed by the upward-looking crowds. It has great formal beauty and an air of mystery. No flash or tripod photographs are allowed. I dive into a group of tourists, jump up on a bench, and take pictures. The uniformed museum employee is fooled, but only for a minute. When she gives me a dirty look and threatens with her index finger, I point innocently to the floor. That stalls her in confusion for a moment; most illegal photographers aim their cameras up toward the great ceiling. I manage to take a few more photos before the guard's patience cracks.

We've underestimated the highway over the pass to Florence in its distance, condition, and steepness. The brakes stink, the mood is strained, our child isn't well, and it's much too cold for Italy. Then on the steepest stretch of the road we run out of gas because I didn't play it safe the last time we tanked up. Ulli says nothing, though what she's thinking is clear enough. On every trip you reach a point like this when you wonder, what am I doing in this town anyway? Why have I asked for all this trouble? Is it just to chase after some dream? I'm in my prime, my friends are making good money, and here I am living on a shoestring, driving around in a camper over hill and dale to look at labyrinths. I'll turn around now. I'll return to my profession, build a little house, and go hiking with my family on weekends. I know I can be very happy this way.

A red-gold sun sets slowly behind the Tuscan landscape. A friendly Italian has picked me up, driven me to a gas station, and brought me back. The spaghetti is steaming, and the wine is spicy. The series of small crises had taken me to the brink of giving up, but the moment has passed. I'm primed anew for Lucca. They've got a very interesting labyrinth there.

17

Closing Circles

The labyrinth of Pavia, Italy, in its original state

You ask:
What, then, is in the center?
Everything

No one knows anymore how or why the labyrinth found its way onto an entrance pillar in front of the cathedral of Lucca. Greeting you at eye level, it has a twenty-inch diameter and is of the same form and age as the labyrinth at Chartres. It's chiseled into a piece of flagstone, so that you can travel the path by finger. Surely, since the thirteen century, millions have done so. I watch two Englishwomen slowly and laughingly trace the old stone furrows with their fingers. Hannah wants to try it as well. I try to decipher the Latin text that accompanies the labyrinth. My labyrinth book helps out:

"Here is the labyrinth that Daedalus of Crete built; no one can escape once inside it. Only Theseus succeeded in doing so, thanks to Ariadne's thread."

I wonder why the church chose to weave the myth of Theseus into its Christian fabric. In the church at Pavia, Theseus is even presented in one line with David and Goliath, as if Theseus were an Old Testament hero. Perhaps I'll know more when I've seen Pavia for myself.

As Hannah travels once more through the labyrinth with her little fingers, I find myself caught up on my old, conditioned ways of thinking. How can no one get out, if there's only one path? The image and the text don't fit; the inscription is illogical. I've grown up in a true-or-false world, where something like this just doesn't fly. But that's because we live in an age of the maze. The architects of Pavia, and all of their predecessors, lived in an age of the labyrinth; for them, apparently, the unity of this image and its text was not problematic. My Gothic angel laughs and says: "There you stand, you educated twentieth-century man, and you just don't get it."

In Pontremoli there's a nearly identical labyrinth. When our labyrinth book was published, the Pontremoli labyrinth was at a temporary location in a castle on a hill overlooking the old city, so it takes a while before we actually find it. It's since been returned to the church of San Pietro, which had been destroyed during a bombing raid in the Second World War. The original church and its adjoining monastery were famous stopping places, historically, for pilgrims on their way to Rome and Santiago de Compostela. A new church has been erected, and the labyrinth stone, the only surviving part of the old structure, has been installed inside it. In the labyrinth's center there's no battle with the Minotaur to be seen, only the Christogram, the Chi-Rho. Here, Christ is the true Theseus, conqueror of the monsters in the labyrinth of our soul. Perhaps it was this parallel that brought Theseus into the church family.

The worn gray stone set into the freshly plastered wall reminds me of the saying: "You can't pour new wine into old wineskins." Perhaps old wines can't be put in new wineskins, either. In Lucca, I could almost hear the sound of the medieval stonemason's chisel; I could see in my daughter's fingers thousands of fingers tracing the same grooves. But here an old stone has been crudely slapped onto a wall that's much too white. It may never tell its stories again until it's been given a place in keeping with its dignity.

We hurry to get to Pavia that same day. The church of San Michele is closed, so we relax in a neighboring café. When we try the church again, the gate is open, and the sexton is just going in with a ladder. I try my bad Italian one more time. Yes, there's a labyrinth up there. Yes, I can have the ladder to get a closer look at it. How many faxes, translations, requests, and confirming telephone calls would it have taken if I'd tried to arrange this in advance? Everything is taken care of in a matter of seconds, and now I'm standing on a shaky nineteen-foot stepladder above what is presumably the oldest walkable church labyrinth in the world. It's worked out in mosaic inlay and, though likely constructed in the first half of the eleventh century, it already shows the Gothic pattern. Unfortunately, part of the labyrinth was destroyed during a sixteenth-century floor renovation. Nevertheless, it still radiates the magic of its history. I learn that a drawing has been preserved from the time when it was still intact; I hope that it will one day be restored.

Our caravan journey has come to its end. We've seen a lot and surely missed a lot as well. We've heard many things and have probably understood little of them. This trip counts among the most beautiful experiences of my life: the journey from labyrinth to labyrinth, from path to path, from center to center.

A few days after our return to Innsbruck yet another circle closes for me. Throughout the trip I'd been searching for a special piece of labyrinth jewelry. I'd gone to countless jewelry and silverworking shops in Strasbourg, London, Glastonbury, Cologne, Ravenna, and Florence. Then in a tiny Indian jewelry shop in Innsbruck I finally locate the piece I've been looking for. The shop is practically facing my own front door.

18

The First Construction

The Dancing James

Whatever life may bring,
don't forget the dance of joy.

— Reinhold Stecher

In Innsbruck they're holding a garden exhibition. I've been invited to lay out a prototype of the labyrinth I'd sketched for the cathedral square here. I use paving stones and flowers. Building labyrinths is always a battle with materials. The challenge is to set up the longest possible path in the smallest possible space. Conditions in the square allow for a labyrinth with a diameter of little more than thirty feet. I need almost five hundred paving stones, and it takes a whole day to lay them down and straighten them out. But I immerse myself in the work, thoroughly enjoying it. Stone by stone, a path is created that slowly takes shape as a whole. Fragments come together to form an image; a painting comes into being on the earth.

When the labyrinth is finished, I want to see it from above. In a nearby school building I find a large stepladder. In the last, fading light I drag the ladder to the labyrinth, and climb up. I'm really satisfied; it looks wonderful, especially from this bird's-eye view — or rather, from the perspective of the angels.

Over the next few days I sit for hours by the labyrinth and watch children and retirees, individuals and groups, men and women enter the path. I begin thinking statistically. Do more men or more women take the route? What percentage of the children who pass by choose to enter in? I even try my hand at slightly more involved calculations: How high is the proportion of men in comparison with women, who, once they've reached the center, don't go back by the return path but directly out? Or, is there any relation between a person's age and the number of repeat trips he or she will make through the labyrinth? But I soon lose interest in scientific methods. No sooner have I formulated a conjecture than it's refuted by what I see. There seem to be no general rules governing the labyrinth, just individual events that reveal more and more of its secrets.

Over time it occurs to me that, more often than not, something special happens to people in the center. I hear a sound of delight or see a radiant face; someone throws up her arms, another bends down.

73

I've made the center of this labyrinth quite small — too small, I soon realize.

The center. The forgotten center. The lost center. The rediscovered center. The gift of the center. I'm almost astonished to realize how little I've thought about this aspect of the labyrinth before. And yet I'm unconsciously searching all the time for the center in my life and in my actions.

The thought occurs to me that my body too must have a center. I run my fingers up and down my chest and abdomen. It takes a long while before I think I can sense the center of my body.

Later I wonder where the center of my apartment is. I have no idea; only days later does it become clear to me, and then I also know why it took me so long to find it. It's the center of our dining room table. I was fooled by its placement, at the extreme outer edge of the apartment. Now it's located more properly, and it marks the symbolic center of our apartment.

There's a center in almost every city as well. Usually it's even marked as such, and has been laid out quite consciously by some city founders on a specific site. Then I read that ancient cultures established a place they called *axis mundi,* the center of the world itself, the point through which the axis of the planet runs.

So often the only paths that become sensible to us are those that lead to a definite center. Otherwise we lack a sense that we've unambiguously *arrived* anywhere. Most of the time something seems to be missing. So much in life is better compared to a string of pearls. Imagine each stone is a small goal along the way. No sooner have you reached one than you see that there's a new one to be attained — the next pearl; and you resume the forward march.

This gradualism has a great disadvantage. If I don't reach a point at which it seems natural to celebrate the goal I've reached, I seldom take the time to give three cheers for what I've achieved. It seems to me that joy might have something to do with discipline — the discipline of pausing to celebrate before rushing on.

But life also has unmistakable moments of arrival: birth, earning a degree, finalizing an agreement, a birthday divisible by ten, retirement, death. These are events in which reaching a center is perceptible to everyone.

In a certain way the trip through a labyrinth approximates these powerful life experiences. The labyrinth is a path without ambiguity. The center of the labyrinth is undivided, without any missing remainder. That seems to be the reason why the center of the labyrinth is so often a place of joy. It's as if one were walking on holy ground. Few are ready to leave this center right away. Many stay there as long as possible.

When I've reached the center, the path I've taken surrounds me. Though I've continuously circled the center, I haven't actually stepped into it until this very moment. Now I have an overview of the whole path; I notice that all sections, all phases of the journey are now perfectly centered. This perfection calms me; the center radiates a great security and satisfaction. It's such a relief, and so beautiful that I can almost believe that my own life and the course of the world are mirrored in it. I catch myself thinking, "This is how I wish things really were!" And yet I sense deeply that it is how things are. I know that our own souls, the earth we inhabit, and the very universe all have a center. Knowledge of the center is an inextinguishable primordial memory. Every person bears this fundamental knowledge inside himself or herself.

I sit on a bench next to the "Dancing James," and arrange my brochures. It's a warm day. The visitors to the garden show won't come till the cool of evening. Half within my field of vision I see my daughter as she walks the labyrinth, totally focused. Having arrived in the middle, she sits down on the center stone, lifts her little hands, and says a single word: "I."

I get goose bumps on the back of my neck, For a moment this little child was sitting in the center of the universe.

19

The Sunwheel

The sunwheel,
in the City Park of Innsbruck

*In the labyrinth we see mirrored
something of the deep truths
of the universe in which we all live.*

A year later I'm once again at the garden show. This time I'm building a different labyrinth. It's a classical Cretan labyrinth, except that I've built it in concentric circles. This time I'd like to have a larger center, and that will work only if I give the circle priority over the square. The square, which is set down over the center of the labyrinth, will lose its shape and turn into a parallelogram.

Circles and squares are bound together in the classical labyrinth as equal in value. If the creator favors one shape over the other, the other suffers. That too is a mirror for many things in our lives.

This time my labyrinth measures thirty-three feet across and has seven paths around the center. I make the demarcation out of flower-beds bordered by wooden palisades. The flowerbeds are planted with yellow and orange flowers, glowing like a sunwheel.

Something special has to be put in the center; a comfortable spot that invites lingering, with lots of soft bark mulch and an unobtrusive bench. But I've been toying with another thought as well. The center is also where the encounter with the Minotaur occurs, a confrontation with the self, the battle with the inner and outer monsters. A mirror would be powerful, perhaps even one bearing the inscription: "This is the Minotaur," as I once saw in a mirror labyrinth. I find a solution that pleases me: I place a bronze disk that shimmers like gold in the center. I do without the inscription. I remember how many of last year's visitors to the labyrinth experienced the center as a benefaction. I don't want to disturb this experience with needless provocation. In this labyrinth, a golden mirror will lie in wait like a little sun. Whoever teaches the center will be greeted by a pleasant warmth, the reflected light of the sky and the real itself.

If I want to, I can always lurk at the entrance and say:

"Go to the center; and when you get there, you will see the Minotaur!"

But of course I don't.

Again I spend hours on a bench next to the labyrinth, watching. A father says with an indulgent smile, "Yes," when his three-year-old son pleads, "Ten more times!"

No one, including myself, would expect that the boy means this number literally. After all, the path to the center and back is over a thousand feet long. By the third time, the father is already starting to lose patience. By the fifth time, he tries to bribe his son away with an ice cream cone. Thank God, he doesn't simply grab the boy. After more than an hour an exhausted, but persistent lad comes for the last time to the exit; his is the glowing face of a hero who has accomplished his task. What is it that has kept him at this task, strenuous as it has been?

In contrast are the adults who give up after the second or third turn and stride out of the labyrinth across the flowerbed. It takes too long for them. One man walks out only a few yards before reaching the center because someone shouts at him, "You'll never find your way in!"

It really hurts to see someone giving up so close to a goal which would be effortlessly reached in a few steps. How often does this happen in life? Many people won't try the labyrinth for fear of losing their way. They can't get past the notion that a labyrinth is really a maze. I've posted a map of the sunwheel at the entrance and written on it in large letters: "You can't get lost here." But that doesn't convince those who fear the possibility of doing something wrong.

Over the course of the exhibition I see many who stand at the edge of the labyrinth, trying to find the center with their eyes or fingers. I see youngsters turning it into a race course. An elegantly dressed man tends some business on his cell phone as he walks. Couples hold hands. Old folks with canes persistently plod the entire length of the narrow path. Many of the children, and even a poodle, seem to take pleasure in the labyrinth. And there are those who surprise me by their familiarity with the labyrinth, those who say, "Oh, yes, this *is* a real labyrinth!"

Soon the labyrinth acquires its regulars: a group of older children who run through it every day on their way by. They help me to water the flowers, and ask me all sorts of questions about the labyrinth. The labyrinth is truly a symbol of all humanity. It knows no boundaries of age, skin color, or profession of faith. It reflects something of the deep truths of the universe in which we all live.

At some point a family from India comes by, and I learn that they too know the labyrinth; several exist near their hometown. I show them my books and pictures of Indian labyrinths. The labyrinths they're familiar with aren't among them. This is neither the first nor the last time that I suspect there are still some undocumented old labyrinths to be discovered in India.

Unfortunately, I cannot undertake a research trip to India right away. But I am resolved to take another trip: to travel soon to Basel, to dig up for myself what already has been documented — Carl Schuster's collected treasures.

20

The Archive in Basel

"Man in the Maze" —
the labyrinth of the Hopi Indians

*The labyrinth leaves a trail running through
the history of the human race
and the most varied cultures of the world.*

S ince I first heard of it, I knew that I would have to go there; now here I am, in the archives of Carl Schuster. My calls to the Ethnology Museum in Basel to set up the visit were of little help. There's a room there where all of Carl Schuster's photos and files are stored, and apparently everything is filed away in an orderly fashion — but so far no one has been able to figure out exactly what Carl Schuster's organizational system was.

"In that short a time, you won't find anything there. We can't let you in alone, and I have no time to stay there with you." Such were the official responses that I got. But in my experience, certain things are better explained face-to-face, and so one day I found myself standing at the door of the museum.

First, I borrow the library's twelve-volume work by Schuster, edited by Ed Carpenter. I discover the section that contains photos and reports of labyrinths from all over the world. The labyrinths of the Hopi Indians in Arizona and the stone labyrinths from the Sonoran Desert in Mexico particularly fascinate me. How did the labyrinth function among the Indians? There are some of Schuster's photos that I'd like to use; I jot down the numbers of the pictures, 221 to 340, and take them to the professor in charge. "You'll see, we won't find it," he says. Still he pulls out the key, marches across the corridor, and opens up the Schuster room. It's small and welcoming, full of filing cabinets and chests of drawers.

"See, the photos filed under the numbers you have are completely different," he says as he pulls out a folder.

"May I look around for an hour? I think I'll find them. Please."

I sense that my hope of seeing the original pictures teeters on a knife's edge. Will he refuse me or not? "I'll find them," I say once more; and he replies: "Good. An hour, at most."

Everything in this room strikes me as perfectly ordered — I just have to figure out the system of logic at work. I pull out a drawer and flip through thousands of negatives. What a fascinating researcher he was, this man who developed such an unusual approach of comparing symbols from far flung cultures. In the course of his inquiries, he collected an unbelievably large amount of photographic material, countless unique treasures. And all this work almost passed away with him.

Of course, I can't look through thirty thousand negatives in an hour. I'll need luck here. I go slowly through the overstuffed drawers. letting my fingers glide over the partitions.

The chapter on labyrinths is found in the center of the tenth volume of the set. I try to get an overview of all the files, and begin to calculate: if the beginning of the material is here, and the end is there, then the photos from the middle of tenth volume must be right around this spot. On tenterhooks I draw the corresponding file out of the cabinet. It contains the photos that are found in the book just before the labyrinths. I put the file back and pick up the next one. All at once I'm filled with the kind of joyful nervous tension that I often feel when I take that last step into the center of labyrinth. I open the file. There they are, I've found them.

The professor comes in and stands amazed: "How'd you do that?"

Apparently knotty problems sometimes get resolved quite simply. Before me lie photos from a strange world. If need be, I can guess at the stories that lie behind them. Were the labyrinths used for rites of initiation? I'm fascinated by the photos of North American Indian labyrinths and stone labyrinths in India. Did the peoples who made these also see the labyrinth as a symbol of life, in which so many basic truths are revealed? Was it used for dances, as in Europe, or for secret rituals? Is its tradition still alive among descendants today? My researcher's heart begins to beat violently, and I already see myself marching though the lonely high desert between Utah and Mexico on a quest for the secret of the labyrinth. Or else I'm riding a motorcycle through India, asking for directions a thousand times, until I stand before the old stone circles and temple engravings.

I choose the most interesting photos and get permission to publish them. I put off the expedition to the Indians, American and otherwise, till later.

21

The Trip to Chartres

Labyrinth in the Chartres cathedral, France

*Many things unfold their beauty
only when seen from above.*

I really don't know why we left Chartres out of our trip through France. It has one of the most celebrated church labyrinths from the Gothic period, the mother of all medieval labyrinths, so to speak. Again and again, from travelers and in books, I've heard stories about this church and its labyrinth. I realize that, in one way or another, everyone who has talked about it has fallen into raptures. Chartres must be a very special place.

But I can't just drive there, walk into the cathedral, join a tour group, photograph the labyrinth, and drive away. I can't treat this place as if it were simply one among many. So I take a whole week. I travel to Paris, and from there I want to go on foot. In Paris I stay the night in a hotel right near the cathedral of Notre Dame. It's the starting point of my trip. It's interesting to hike out of a large city. First, there's the old city, then the middle-class neighborhoods, then blocks of concrete, then the suburbs. In between are mall parks, light industry, and lots of cars. I've never experienced the organism of a large city in this fashion. With almost surprising suddenness I leave the city behind me and find myself in a silent forest. The hiking is pleasant, as paths through woods and fields feed into little bits of street and then back again. I pass by Versailles; for a time all the roads are perfectly straight, then once again they get less rigid, with gentle curves and turns.

On the fourth day I walk toward an iron cross, which stands alone in a large wheat field on a slightly raised stretch of ground. I sense what this means and feel a rising tension and joy within me. I've guessed right. When I reach the cross, I see for the first time the cathedral of Chartres looming up just a little above the wheat field. It's still a long way off, a good twelve miles; but my heart is lighter, and so are my feet and backpack.

For a long while I walk along a river valley. Finally I climb the many steps to the hilltop on which stands the only Gothic cathedral that has never gone through any major changes or damage. Over

80 percent of the stained-glass windows still survive from its original thirteenth-century glazing.

I've been sitting for less than five minutes, sweaty and happy, outside the grille in front of the entrance, when someone greets me in German. A pastor whom I know is here with a travel group. They're just now beginning one of the quite rare "guided-air-tours," during which visitors walk on the paths constructed inside the façade for the original glaziers and masons. I'm allowed to join in—what a felicitous meeting! Before I even set foot inside the cathedral, I will experience it from the outside, from as close up as any human can. I am amazed at so much—the buttress technique, the beauty of all the fine details.

The leader shows us figures that can't be seen from any spot on the ground. The master builders created a work of art whose totality would, first and foremost, give honor to God, and only secondarily bring joy and edification to human beings. God, as every knows, sees all things. I press my nose against a colorful stained-glass window and take away a silhouette-like impression of the interior, as our guide explains the window's unique methods of manufacture.

Now comes something completely unexpected: we're continuing our tour up into the vaulted roof. After a fire the roof was reinforced with a steel structure. I'm aware of the beating of my heart. I know that in the arch under the wooden staircase there is a hole almost directly above the labyrinth. From there you can look down on the labyrinth from 120 feet in the air. A French tour guide walks by, a clutch of keys in his hand, at the rear of a group of tourists. I accost him and ask whether I'd be allowed to climb down and take a look, perhaps even a picture. He must sense how important to me this glimpse through the hole is.

When the group has disappeared into the narrow staircase of the towers, I'm allowed to climb down a small ladder and then walk out onto the topside of the vault. The guide checks whether there is anything on me that might fall out when I bend over the hole. With a serious smile he says:

"If you drop anything, you'll be the last one ever permitted to look through it."

Then he draws away the wooden cover over the hole. I'm so excited I tremble. Then I look down. The labyrinth lies beneath me like a golden medallion. Seen perpendicularly from above, people look like ants. I sink into a moment of intense observation, out of which I'm pulled all too soon by the tapping foot of the tour guide. We have to rejoin the group.

Fascinated observation once more turns into trembling excitement when I have to wedge the camera from out beneath my belly. I check three times to make sure the strap is around my neck. The exposure time is long, and my hands won't hold steady. All the photos that I take will turn out blurry; but this picture of the labyrinth will always remain sharp and clear inside me.

22

The Navel of the World

Modern labyrinth

*The labyrinth
is humanity's
first center,
the middle of the gut,
the navel of the world.*

"**D**o you want to join us tomorrow for meditation in the lower church?" my friend, the pastor, asks me. I like the idea. I enter the cathedral this time through the lower outside entrance. The candle-filled lower church with its well and Black Madonna, dating from pre-Christian druidic times, strikes me as a strong foundation for the cathedral above. I know that, like Chartres, Christian churches were often built over older, pre-Christian sites; but in Chartres everything seems to have twice as strong an effect as elsewhere.

When I'm back above ground and ready to enter the interior of the church, I fall in with a guided tour on its way to the west portal. The guide, an Austrian specialist on Chartres who has been living here for twenty years, impresses me. His commentary combines scholarship and myth, understanding of symbolism and history, in a way that seems both effortless and ingenious. After I have listened to his lecture on the portal, I tag along with the group into the interior.

"All the proportions here were chosen deliberately. As one moves forward down the cathedral's main aisle, one finds that the distances between the gate and the labyrinth, the labyrinth and the center of the crossing (where the arm of the cross, or transept, intersects the aisle), and the crossing and the center of the altar are exactly equal. These three areas symbolize, when transposed to the human body, the gut, heart and head. Anyone who walks forward from the back of the cathedral, is, as it were, walking through a body. The altar stands in the center of the head; that is, the place of understanding and knowing. A lot of people today want to know everything all at once in order to arrive immediately at the altar of faith. But the mystery of faith can be understood only by those who have first worked through their emotions, contemplated their lives, and turned around or repented. Afterward they have to step into their heart and open it to the fullest. And only then can they understand what is going on at the altar. That is the message that was built into these stones."

It's fascinating to note how the Gothic master builders seem to have thought everything through. I again discover a new aspect of the labyrinth: the labyrinth as a sign of the gut, as the navel of the world.

I've heard this before, somewhere. Still, I've always thought of the labyrinth as something first of all for the feet, and then for the head; a symbol to be experienced bodily and then thought through and understood. But, the gut? The gut is where the emotions get processed, "cooked"; where power and violence are at home, along with our aggressions and lusts.

In my imagination I let the labyrinth sink into my gut, into the twists of the intestines. Everything has to be churned and mixed together there, until what is nourishing separates from what is useless. From all that I take in, the gut separates the good, which turns into "life force," from the bad, which is cast aside as waste. Looked at in this way, the work of the gut is important in all realms of life, most especially where good and evil lie side by side. I'd say that the domains of power, aggression, and sexuality belong primarily to the gut.

Again I take joy in the untroubled holism expressed in Gothic art. A third of the church belongs to the gut. For a long time pilgrims were allowed to spend the night in this part of the church; and at least early on, the sexes were not expected to sleep on separate sides of the church, as they later were (women on the left, men on the right). I am amazed at the variety of things, through the ages, that have been permitted in church buildings. And why not? I'd actually like to do that too sometimes, perhaps only to express with my body what I believe in my head, namely that sexuality belongs to God's good work of creation. Many would probably find that disturbing. But I'm sure of one thing; it wouldn't disturb "the Master of the house."

The barriers are taken down; it's time to enter onto a path that was laid out here eight hundred years ago in order to open people to the mysteries of life's path, to initiate and teach them in its ways.

"For you, this must surely be something altogether special," a woman acquaintance remarks to me. But if you watch too intently for what's special to occur, it doesn't turn up. My path through the labyrinth remains sober till the end. I know that after the early pilgrims to Chartres had reached the center of its labyrinth, they went straightaway to the center of the cathedral's crossing. I do the same.

"Here is the place in the cathedral where the light comes in evenly from all sides. That means that all shadows dissolve," the guide had said. You can no longer go into the absolute center of the crossing, because now the altar which faces the congregation stands there. I remain standing in front of the altar kneeler and involuntarily stretch out my arms upward. My fingers point to the north and south rose windows. I sense a freedom in my heart, exalted in the light of the church. Here is the place where I'm finally allowed to touch the holy. The moment is indescribable. Although today the labyrinth has fallen silent, God has not.

The area of the church where the altar stands is reserved for people taking part in the liturgy. This part of the church interests me the least. I have to go back to "my" labyrinth. I sit in front of it; it's just now being closed off again, as it regularly is, to keep the labyrinth walkers from blocking the flow of tourists. But I don't let myself be deterred by the closing. I crawl around on the floor for two hours. In the center stone of the labyrinth iron nails have been driven in, making a strange form. They're supposed to have once served to fasten down a long-gone copper plate, but nobody knows their origin for sure. Before the trip one of my friends had told me that he didn't believe the theory of the plate, since there are iron nails driven in throughout the entire labyrinth. I am now in search of these nails, and I sketch their positions into a graphic of the labyrinth. I'm mystified by the unusual arrangement and the varying sizes of the nails. Were they meant to represent the shape of a star? In the nineteen century, the floor plates in the middle of the labyrinth were raised to see if anything lay beneath them. Nothing was found, but the nails from the disturbed section have certainly been lost. So I have here a difficult puzzle, from which as many as half the pieces may be missing. To this day I have no answer to the puzzle of the nails.

Early the next day I'm back in the cathedral. I observe people who walk through the church and over the labyrinth without even noticing this strange path underfoot. But I see others absorbed in it: a couple of newlyweds stand in the center; a nun kneels down in the center; young girls walk hand in hand; and a woman dancer seems to fly through the path on the tips of her toes. Meanwhile a man stands along the side and traces the lines with his fingers.

More and more groups of tourists arrive, and a guard whom I call the "closer-upper" ends this session of labyrinth walking. For hours I amble through the gigantic interior of the cathedral. There aren't many churches in which one can spend an entire day, but in Chartres, for all its nobility and grandeur, I find a very livable atmosphere. Nothing here crushes or depresses me. Perhaps the builders of this church knew something about how to put together a good place for the soul. They left nothing out, they did nothing halfway, and they ignored nothing. They certainly knew a great many things that are lost arts today.

I bow in all directions to the artisans, the glaziers, the stonemasons, and the architects, as well as to the man who thought of putting in the labyrinth. In the middle of my slow farewell to this wonderful house, somebody asks:

"Do you want to go up one more time?"

I can hardly take in my good fortune. The leader is taking me and four others up again to the vault. This time I'm no longer in a state of excitement, but simply happy to once again look down on the golden medallion, the navel of the world. And this time the photos come out sharp and clear.

23

A Trip through the Ages

Former dancing ground
in Kaufbeuren, Germany

The labyrinth awakens the desire
to put it to fresh use
again, and again,
to weave it into our stories, games, and dances.
It awakens the desire
to apprehend the universal truths
that lie hidden in these seemingly simple lines.

The labyrinth had an important place in Gothic art. It was placed at the very center of the first part of the cathedral. It was a path in initiation, a path of pilgrimage. In the early Gothic Easter rituals it was used as a dancing ground, much as the classical labyrinth was used almost three thousand years earlier. For three hundred years this Easter dance was a customary component of the annual liturgy. Then it disappeared. In the eighteenth century, numerous labyrinths were torn out of European churches. Then, near the end of the nineteenth century, a small number of church labyrinths were once again built. For another hundred years the labyrinth remained dormant; but now there's another revival of interest in it. What are the reasons for this strange journey of the labyrinth itself though the ages?

The Gothic mind sought to find an architectonic expression for everything known and believed. Its animating concern was a desire for completeness. Everything was at stake, all knowledge, all life, all faith; gut, heart, and head. After the Gothic period came the sixteenth-century age of the written word and the printed book. Then came humanism, the Reformation, and later the Enlightenment. As the word became authoritative, people began to place an unprecedented importance on making precise distinctions between things; on dividing things into parts, and distinguishing true from false. Today we live at the zenith and end of this age. The word has been multiplied to infinity. The Internet delivers virtually anything and everything to your desk: a true "information overload." In the last five hundred years of our western culture, the head has been granted a dominating significance. The heart was neglected, the gut ignored. There was no more dancing in the labyrinth; the navel of the world was ripped out.

This attitude may be clearly seen and felt in the modern-day cathedral of Chartres. In the "head" of the church stands the main altar. Decorated with a monumental marble structure (*The Assumption of Mary into Heaven* dating from the eighteen century), it is easily understandable that this altar is mentioned in the guidebooks to the church. The privileged realm of the head is safeguarded against unwanted visitors. It's as if the clergy have barricaded themselves behind it. The "heart," the center of the crossing, where the light is perfectly balanced and the shadows dissolve, is a place you can't enter anymore. Some years ago the altar *coram populo* had been built there: after all, the Second Vatican Council wanted the Church to move more into the heart — the quintessentially right choice for the future. In Chartres, however, the "altar facing the people" looks rather orphaned. Mass is celebrated there only on high feast days. The prophetic power of Vatican II has not yet unfolded its whole effect.

The "gut," however, is the outright problem child of the cathedral. For years it has been covered with chairs — that no one sat on. Ultimately, requests from all over the world to open up the labyrinth to walkers could no longer be resisted. Now the chairs are removed from the labyrinth one day a week. I asked a responsible clergyman why they do not open it all the time if so many people love to walk it. He answered me reproachfully, "We are still a church." When you enter the section of the altar you pass a little sign that says: Reserved for prayers! Not many people are there. But on Fridays (when the labyrinth is open) the church is filled with heartily praying people. Why are those who walk the labyrinth such a threat to the clergy? I can almost hear them thinking, "We'd really like to tear this thing out, if only the historical preservation society would let us." The gut and the Church have a hard time getting along.

The Catholic Church's conflicts with power and sexuality are captured more aptly in the image of the maze, where all is threatening and frightful, fateful and uncertain. Complex questions, to the extent possible, are divided neatly into "correct" and "incorrect" answers. If the "gut" and all the human elements that belong to it were re-imaged in the form of the labyrinth, much of the tension we feel in the Church and in society could be loosened.

24

Just Get It Right

Sketch for a garden labyrinth

The labyrinth doesn't ask:
Are you going the right way or the wrong way?
The labyrinth asks
Are you going?

L ife in Central European culture is very strictly oriented to the principle: Right is good, wrong is bad. Anyone who reaches a wrong decision has made an unnecessary detour; he or she is wasting valuable time. And now something might happen that can't be fixed! This worldview is represented graphically in the maze. One who winds up on a dead-end street has taken a useless trip. The person who get through the maze "best" is the one who makes the fewest mistakes and finds the right route as quickly as possible. Our education system, too, is based on this principle. The key is to make a few errors as possible. On examinations given in Germany serious mistakes get two red marks, minor mistakes get one. Grades are generally calculated on the basis of the total number of mistakes marked. With painful precision, students are trained, for a period of nine to twelve years, to get everything right. Nothing is more important in schools than to come as close as possible to the Answer — which the teacher provides.

School is designed to prepare pupils for the world. And in the world that grown-ups face many things *are* organized and set up in accordance with a strict and complicated system of "true" and "false."

In this cultural context, the labyrinth sends us an astonishing message. It says: "The question of true-or-false is unimportant." The crucial question is a different one: "To go or to stay put?" In the labyrinth the path is always the right one, even when one of its turns lead away from the center. In the labyrinth there's no longer or shorter way. Every turn must be taken; nothing can be omitted if you want to get to the center. But for the person who is willing to learn from the turns in the path, who doesn't freeze in panic, mistakes are transformed from time squandered into precious stretches of road traveled. Wounds become places of healing, crises lead to renewed life force, and errors to wisdom.

It's not wrong to make mistakes. A mistake is neither dead end nor time lost. The real error in life is to fail to learn from mistakes; to stay put when one could go on.

I have become very skeptical of the saying, "Just get it right." This precept can function as a curse, making people hesitant, or even bringing them to a dead halt on their path. How often people suffer from the fact that others are always telling them what to do and how to do it. All too often we are confronted with the requirement of doing things differently—and, hence, "right."

The labyrinth frees us from the compulsion to continuously seek the right path. It sets me free to be the way I am. I have to travel my own distinctive path, and I have to traverse every turn in my labyrinth in order to get to the center.

When someone asks me, "What's the right way to walk through a labyrinth?" I always answer, "There's no right way or wrong way to go through a labyrinth. Whichever way you go, it's the right way." It's not possible to go too slowly or too quickly; there's no "two steps forward and one step back"; no attitude too open or too reticent; no better or worse path to the center. The path is taken; or it is not.

For me the labyrinth is an invitation to trust that my life has both followed and is continuing on a good path. We can take the prevailing directives—"*This* is the way to do it right"—and lay them aside. I don't accept that my life is locked into a bewildering maze, with someone sitting in judgment behind every wrong turn mocking my stupidity. I believe in a path that I take in just the way I'm taking it. I ultimately believe in the great contradiction, the great paradox, the great mystery of life: that on one hand I am as a person utterly free, that I may be entirely myself, unique and irreplaceable; and that at the same time I am perfectly secure and led, completely embedded in a sure path. The labyrinth is not a path that constricts me. Rather, it's one that grants me freedom from the need to reinvent my own life's path, while offering me freedom to walk it in a way unlike anyone before or after me.

25

The Limits of Words

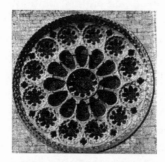

Western rose window in Chartres

*Some sermons
are best
when no words are said*

I am sitting in front of the west portal of the cathedral in Chartres wondering when I'll come here again. I look by turns at the stone figures and then the people who are the last to exit at closing time. Half the world is reflected in their different skin colors and facial features. Over the entrance door the story of Jesus is depicted: his birth, his life journey, and his promised return at the end of time. My eyes wander over the portal, which is slowly being dipped in the evening light. The west rose window glows above me like a gigantic flower.

I admire the architects of Chartres in their meticulous attention to detail. The distance from the floor beneath the west entrance door to the center of the rose window above it is 107 feet, exactly the distance from the entrance to the center of the labyrinth as well. But that's not all. The size of the west rose window exactly matches the size of the labyrinth. At the center of this west window of the Resurrection is Christ surrounded by apostles and angels; in the circle around them are represented the risen faithful. The path of the human being that is expressed in the paths of the labyrinth has its corresponding expression in the Resurrection window. The labyrinth and the window would fit neatly as overlays, one on top of another. On high, behind the humans who are traveling their labyrinthine life paths, the window gleams like a lasting reminder that after this life our earthbound state will be dissolved, and we will be taken into the Resurrection.

I love these messages that only images can convey. There are many things that I can't put into words to match the way I know them inside myself. There is so much in life for which language is not the appropriate means of communication. Perhaps that's one reason why the labyrinth is undergoing a seeming renaissance in the human consciousness. There are enough good words, sermons, and explanations — but few verbal messages can unfold within us the fullness of their power and meaning. The labyrinth, the stained-glass window — all architecture expresses things for which words are not adequate. A symbol is like a secret world language that's understood by everyone, regardless of what mother tongue or worldview you've grown up with.

The train carries me into the darkness of the night. The smells are different, the speed, the light. Without holy places in our memory, without the revelations of pictures and symbols, life would be dreary and flat, but as it is the radiance of Chartres is still glowing over my soul.

26

Absolutely Certain

Silver coin from Crete

*Anyone who thinks
that anything in life
is completely controllable
has become a stranger
to the cultures of the world.*

The experiences I had at Chartres stay with me. I ask myself, what happened to central European culture after the Gothic period? What brought an end to the Easter dance that the bishop once shared with priests in the labyrinth? After the French Revolution the Cathedral of Chartres was used as a temple of the goddess Reason. The representatives of the church did come back some thirty years later, but it seems they never fully regained possession of the place from which they'd been driven out. The church certainly didn't reinstate the dance; in some places the old dance floor, the labyrinth, was even deliberately destroyed. Important parts of the formerly integrated whole were ignored and eradicated, and the goddess Reason remained on her throne.

The head, in whose center the altar stands, is something of great value. Reason brings clarity, orientation, and order. Reason generates certainty. But without the heart and gut to ground it, reason becomes distant and cold—and often deceptive as well.

We have a basic human need for certainty. We want as much in life as possible to be definite. We anchor ourselves as much as we can in a fixed system of habits, which provides us orientation. And then when something new comes along, as it inevitably will, we urgently seek certainty in dealing with it, even though we know that there are no guarantees of safety when dealing with the unknown.

This desire for certainty can also make the path in the labyrinth difficult. First it swings to the left, then to the right. Everything changes— perspective, direction, movement. What was hitherto clear may now no longer be relevant; something that had finally come into perspective may no longer make sense. But if I'm forced, mid-course, to give up something familiar that I've relied on to get where I am, I'll be willing to accept the change as long as its clear that it's helping me to move forward. I'll want this turn in the path to at least lead me inward, toward the center. But if the turn instead leads outward, I become frustrated. Can this be right? The longing for what I'm used to grows. I get vexed with a world that won't stand still.

My uncertainty swells when I experience a major turn in my life or have to take many turns in rapid succession. What still holds true for me now, and what doesn't? What is irretrievably past, and what is just beginning? In this fog of uncertainty I easily lose sight of the big picture. I fasten my gaze on the ground in front of my feet, and cannot see beyond them. Sometimes I'm afforded a pause. I have time to look up and survey my surrounds. Then the gnawing question pops up: "What have I gotten myself into?" I sense how much has already escaped me in my myopia, sometimes even the goal that I had originally set out for.

Deeply rooted in our soul is the desire to see clearly what our goals are, to grasp hold of the reins, to maintain control. To know that such and such a thing is certain — absolutely certain. How many people have already spoken those last two words? Technicians, politicians, husbands, scientists — most often it is a man with a serious look on his face who uses these words and does not realize how much he is relying on beliefs and hopes.

I recall a sign at my school, back in the 1970s, about atomic energy. It read: *Atomic energy is the safest available way to generate energy. The likelihood of a major accident is so small that is may practically be excluded.*

Every person harbors the naïve wish for absolute security, especially in areas of life where the risks are incalculable. But whatever the issue — be it atomic energy or genetic engineering, relationships or the path we take — life is fragile, the soul is restless. And even the planet Earth, spinning so reliably around the sun, is ultimately vulnerable as well.

In the long run life spares no one the experience of its vulnerable edges. The outside paths of the labyrinth symbolize these borders, which we experience as sickness, accidents, death, a life's work that has collapsed, a dream that has dissolved. Often the connections are incomprehensible and depressing. Many "whys?" are never answered: we are left empty-handed knowing that the world is not ours to grasp.

I'm comforted in knowing that, even in an uncertain world, I can feel secure; even in the most uncertain times, I can believe that I am in the firm hands of God.

27

The Wheel of Fire

Tattoo pattern from Brazil

Light overcomes immeasurable distances,
giant spaces, and the deepest darkness.
Light is the proof
that something very small
can have a great effect.

More and more often I find myself wondering what would be the effect of a labyrinth built with candles. For the feast of St. Martin in November my daughter's kindergarten class always present a feast of light. That's where I want to build the light labyrinth. First, I consider how best to protect the tea light candles from the wind. For a single candle I can think of plenty of solutions, but not for two hundred. Ground torches are an expensive alternative, but I don't care; I want to see a beautiful labyrinth. With string and a screwdriver I scratch out circles in the grass. Then I set up the torches a stride apart along the circular lines. Finally, I take out my sketch of the labyrinth and install the path and its turns. Shortly before darkness arrives, the labyrinthine wheel of fire is burning. Once again I am astounded: how can a few circular lines have such a powerful effect?

A child stands in the center, then she runs out and gets her mother.

"I want you to take me in there," she says.

Then both stand in the center together; and the child's eyes turn up to the stars and down to the torches. Again and again she lifts her hands and slowly lets them drop, as if the stars were raining down their light.

A father presses my hand and says, "Thanks."

He seems to be looking for more words, but then he walks away. I don't know what moved him so. All at once a chain of children and parents forms spontaneously. More join in and march the path of the labyrinth together through the dark, bright night.

The next year at Easter I'm given the opportunity to lay out a labyrinth of lights in the square in front of my church. On Easter night meditative music and readings take place till dawn. Groups of people from the nearby city center continually drop by. I discuss the labyrinth with teenagers, laugh with tourists, observe impatient parents whose children refuse to leave, speak with a teacher about the re-discovery of wordless teaching. I relight torches that have gone out, and hope that the cold wind won't pick up.

Then I hear a soft voice nearby.

"I don't think I can come back next year, but I'm quite contented now. You've given me a wonderfully beautiful experience this evening. Thanks so much."

I look into the face of a young, frighteningly thin woman and realize that she was speaking about her death. She vanished like a breath of air.

I think of all the vexation I've gone through: setting up the candles, wicks that were too thin to stand up to the wind, carting my materials from the fifth floor storage room, the broken elevator, the wrong address printed on the program, the fact that I wasn't allowed to drill a hole for the midpoint of the measuring string or to let wax drip onto the cobblestone, the fire department permit I couldn't get, and the finances, which were shaky till the last minute. All that too has vanished like a breath of air.

When I return to the labyrinth, there's nobody there. I walk to the entrance, glad that a moment has come when I can walk it undisturbed. First, I try to think about something or other. I say a prayer, then I feel myself quieting inside. I let myself be led. I circle near to the center, then I steadily move with the labyrinth back toward the outside. All at once, a few steps before the last outward turn, I have to stop.

"There you are now," an inner voice says to me.

I look about. "Just go around the curve," another part of me says persuasively.

I don't like having another outward turn to complete. I want to be past it, closer to the center. I know that my voice is right: you can't force this, you can't be further along than you are. I remain standing there, waiting for the inner green light to move ahead. It doesn't come.

"Letting go": I know that something important is contained in this phrase. But I still don't really like it. I want to gain something, to have more than I had yesterday. I don't want to let go. Still, something won't let me move on. I'm being challenged to accept the fact that this is the spot where I am, even though before me lies yet another outward turn. I give up my resistance; I must let go. I take a little piece of paper that I find in my pants pocket, and put it on the spot where I'm standing. I step over the candles and climb out the labyrinth. I remember the prayer I went off with, the question I took to the center. I hadn't expected such a quick answer—nor such a clear one.

28

The Voice of the Heart

Decorative angel on the outer façade
of Watt's Chapel, England

Trusting is dangerous,
hard,
and indispensable.

It's beautiful when people can entrust themselves wholeheartedly to their path, as a river to its bed. Why, then, do I find it so hard to trust — I who am so sure that this is the royal road of life? The river, too, takes its detours. It never really runs straight; it doesn't course around a center, because its center is the sea. It's fascinating to watch how water holds unwaveringly to its path. It's full of an unbridled energy that drives it forward. No stone, no bridge support, no dam can stop it. It circumvents the obstacle, without for a moment losing its headlong impetus. When it occasionally curls into a whirlpool or cove, that seems a perfectly natural pause, a welcome rest; the water emerges again to give itself completely to its path. I know that to achieve this complete trust would mean complete happiness.

Sometimes when I'm on the road as a pilgrim, I try to practice this trust. I like to travel without maps or detailed directions. I take the first steps and try to enter the mindset of trusting that the path will lead me. I don't know the best name to put to this: intuition, the voice of the heart, my inner voice; but I do know that it's a highly reliable guide. At almost every crossroads I reach, it has a definite opinion about which fork to take, as if it were familiar with the land that lies beyond. Sometimes when this voice falls silent, though, I begin to doubt the wisdom of relying on its guidance. I could at least have taken a map along for times like this, I reprimand myself. At such times every step that takes me closer to the crossroads heightens my displeasure: I don't enjoy running into dead ends. But then something almost always happens. If my inner voice isn't sure which path to take, heaven sends me a messenger. A farmer drives by, a child runs out of a house, or a previously concealed road sign gives me the direction I need. Sometimes, of course, though rarely, I do take a totally wrong turn. But that's part of the process. Then I know that I still have a lot to learn.

Water pursues its course in marvelous perfection; the pilgrim pulls this off only occasionally. Even harder is bringing this level of trust into my everyday life. In those brief times that I succeed, moments of astonishment and happiness arise. I experience how simply and well everything develops; suddenly things seem to be working out on their own. Yet, for all that, I don't manage to maintain this serene sense of flow very long. Sooner or later I snap back into more habituated attitudes; I take charge, busy myself, use force, bring my influence to bear, manipulate, manage, sell myself. Isn't this the pathway to success? That's what I've learned, and suddenly I find myself spinning headlong down that track again.

There are messengers who try to save me from myself. They stand by the side of this fast track. Sometimes I clearly recognize them. I can see that they've been sent to me. But I can't deal with them right now. I've already committed my time; I can't change my plans. I hurry on past them. My body and my inner voice try to tell me what's going on, but I haven't really learned to listen to them. Perhaps that's why I've made the labyrinth my focus of interest, with the pilgrimage to Santiago de Compostela my greatest dream, and the saying in Matthew, "Seek first God's kingdom and all these things shall be yours as well," my guiding scriptural verse. Trust in life, trust in my path, trust in God. Anyone who can trust the way water does must be quite close to heaven.

29

The Path Back

The pilgrim in the labyrinth of life

The path to the goal
is the path of the hero
The path to home
is the path of love.

I hear that a pastor of a little Protestant church in the Allgäu region of southern Germany has had a labyrinth built in his chancel. The trip isn't long, and I soon pay him a visit to see this unusual piece of work. Poured from colorful concrete, the labyrinth is light yellow with reddish speckles, on a blue background. The small chancel is completely filled by this little labyrinth, with its seven circuits. At the center of the labyrinth, under a glass cover, lies a stone shaped like a cross. The pastor found this stone on the path to the shrine of St. James of Compostela in Spain.

Over a period of seven years he and his wife have been traveling, stage by stage, the path from his vicarage to Santiago. He tells me some of his pilgrimage experiences, about the dog that accompanied them for a while and led them to a hidden chapel; about the people they met along the way; and about the sign over the till at a hostel in Spain: "Give what you can, take what you need." That's the kind of trust that develops among fellow pilgrims.

Then he shows me a postcard that a good friend of his had later sent him from Spain; it reads, "You have to take the path on your own, and you have to do it all in one stretch."

The sentence arrests me. I was planning to take the path to St. James in stages myself, along with my wife and daughter. It's hardly practical, and certainly not fair to my family, to take my leave and go off alone for half a year on a pilgrimage. Still, I know that the postcard writer is right. And he doesn't even tell the whole story. I know that something else needs adding: You have to take the path alone, you have to do it all in one stretch, and *you have to take it back*.

The question of the path back is essential to the labyrinth. The labyrinth that Daedalus built on Crete as a hiding place for the Minotaur was never — not once — represented in antiquity as a maze, but always as a labyrinth, which has a single path that leads both to the center and back out again. Why, then, does Theseus, who finds the path to the center easily enough, need a thread to find his way back out? Perhaps it helps to remember that myths and fairy tales describe not external realities, but rather internal onces. I'd be only too glad to know what Ariadne's thread means in this inner, symbolic sense. One statement puts me on the track: "It's easier for a man to head off in quest of heroism than in quest of love."

With decisive, concentrated energy, Theseus throws himself into his heroic adventure. He advances single-mindedly upon the monster and destroys it. He's a flawless hero, a tremendous man. And perhaps he would have rushed off to complete a next heroic deed just as single-mindedly, had Ariadne not given him a thread that drew him to love. Her love, after all, is what made his heroic deed possible. Only through Ariadne's intervention could he have conquered the monster. Theseus chooses to be led back by this thread, this love — even though he later will abandon Ariadne. Great heroes don't necessarily make great lovers. Love, though, is always the higher goal. It's the most precious thing to be gained, the only thing that makes life worthwhile.

In a sense, the labyrinth has two paths: the path in and the path out. Two fitting names for these paths now occur to me. I call the way in "the path of the hero," and the path out "the path of love." The way in the path to the center, is the path toward a goal I want to reach. But what good is a goal if I haven't won it in my heart, if it doesn't lead me back to love?

On a pilgrimage one is likewise moving toward a particular goal — the holy place. Some people who have walked the many miles to Santiago or to Rome speak of a great inner emptiness on the day after the triumph. Many climb aboard a train or plan, returning home by the most direct path available — just as some who walk the labyrinth exit straight out from the center. Perhaps these sojourners rob themselves of the path back.

Anyone who has journeyed to Santiago or another place of pilgrimage encounters the Holy, the Extraordinary thee. Such pilgrims have drawn strength from a spiritual wellspring; they have sensed their inner connection to God and the wandering people of humanity. They have traveled for hours, perhaps days, toward this goal, and directed all their thoughts and longings toward it. They have stretched an inner thread from their hearts to this spot and have followed it to their desired end. The thread is rewound and the goal achieved.

The center of the labyrinth is the only place where I have to make a complete turnaround. This turn redirects my eyes to the place from which I came. If I have appreciated the center, if I've taken into myself all that it gives, if I have touched the Sacred — (and in Santiago this is expressed very concretely, as pilgrims lay their hands on the shoulder of the statue of the Apostle James) — then I turn around and head for home. Now I cast forth the inner thread from my heart anew and tie it to the door of my own home. The place of pilgrimage fades from my field of vision; family, friends, and the tasks at home make their way into my heart and thoughts. This path back home should neither be skipped nor shortened; in fact, it may well be the more important part of the journey. Having drawn new strength from achieving the goal, one is newly energized for the return home. The path back is a time for the experience of the sacred to begin finding its place among the experiences of everyday life. It is good to think as much of the people dear to you and of your own simple place in the everyday routine, as you do of the Extraordinary, the Higher, and the Sacred.

On this return path, important things happen. Questions pop up: "What do the people near to me really mean to me? What's my actual task in life?" These questions may lead me so far that I notice my home isn't where I thought it was, that my tasks in life are completely different from what I thought they were. The thread that cast homeward will draw my heart to the place where I truly belong. The labyrinth guides my feet where they must go. I can trust this thread of my heart, even if it should still take more strange twists and turns.

Not till you have seized hold of the doorknob and embraced all that you love have you really arrived home.

30

Labyrinthine Tales

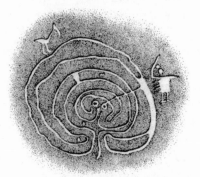

Three-thousand-year-old rock carving
from the Val Canonica, Italy

*God also writes crooked
in straight lines.*

The labyrinthine path is a classic theme. Before a hero's central life task is discovered, he or she will have survived many twists and turns in the road. Perhaps the story most closely tied to the labyrinth is that of Theseus and Ariadne. The labyrinth appears twice here, not just as the prison which holds the Minotaur, but also as the dancing ground on which Theseus and Ariadne celebrate their freedom. This dance was performed for centuries throughout the Mediterranean basin; and traces of it can be found today in various traditional folk dances. The story of Theseus is a tale of a young man's passage into adulthood, his path from youth to king. To complete this path, Theseus must pass through certain states; there are certain steps he must take, or, to follow the metaphor of the labyrinth, a series of turns he must negotiate, before he can become king of Athens. Certain of these events represent necessary stages in the universal process of growing up. They are timelessly valid.

First, Theseus makes his decision to face the challenge. Fearlessly and, in truth, without much reflection, he volunteers to be one of the hostages taken to Crete to be sacrificed to the monster, the Minotaur. Only the person who sets out to win a kingdom can become a king; the myths and fairy tales of the world tell us this a hundred times over.

Just as intrepidly, Theseus strides into the depths of the labyrinth to do battle with the Minotaur. This is the next stage that must be mastered: the struggle with the Evil One. But even his victorious struggle does not yet bring him to his goal. The hero must take on the feminine—in his own soul and in a meeting with woman. The heroic deed is incomplete if love too is not won. Theseus picks up the thread that returns him to Ariadne and thus finds his way to love.

On the journey back a great feast is celebrated. That too is one of the markers of maturity — being able to celebrate life, to enjoy a feast, a party. Later, we know, Theseus leaves Ariadne. The story doesn't make it altogether clear whether she was taken from him or if he abandoned her. Finding a partner, male or female, is often a labyrinthine quest in itself. One seldom finds the right one the first time around.

Finally, before Theseus can become king, he must somehow take the place that his father holds. This happens in a tragic way for Theseus; his father, Aegeus, believing his son to be dead, hurls himself from a cliff into the sea. The overcoming of the father can take many forms, but it must occur in some way if a man is to reach adulthood.

Every one of us has a personal story that's unfolding in a labyrinth of life. This image of the labyrinth helps me to better understand certain epochs and events in my own life as stages along life's way. I can see the points of descent and ascent on my path; where I've turned away from the center, and then found my way toward it again; where I've dealt with turnings; and my ever-present longing for the center which I've understood, at times, as the goal to be reached, and at other times as the halfway point of my journey.

I am sure there are an infinite number of stories, whether immortalized in writing or simply experienced, in which the labyrinth can be glimpsed, in part or whole.

There's one ancient biblical story where I find the theme of the labyrinth especially striking. It's the Old Testament tale of Jonah.

Jonah first hastens away from the city Nineveh, the very place where God has sent him. After many turns—one through the belly of the whale—Jonah finally accepts his path to Nineveh. There he challenges the evils of the city, and indeed overcomes them. But there's a third stretch of the path awaiting Jonah. He leaves Nineveh and walks into the wilderness. In labyrinthine fashion, Jonah's path has first led away from the center, then toward the center, and finally out of the labyrinth.

At first Jonah resists the task that has been laid upon him, and he runs away from the goal. In the course of his flight he falls into a deep crisis, left to die in the open sea. Saved by grace and the belly of a whale, Jonah's path turns again to the center, and he accomplishes his task brilliantly. Through his preaching, an entire city is converted from its evil ways; Jonah's a hero. Nevertheless, he has yet to reach his final goal. Jonah's task is not to be the most successful prophet in the ancient world, but to find his way out of rage and resistance to a sincere inner love. To find acceptance, and a benevolent empathy with the whole of Creation.

God gently sends Jonah on his return path, the path out of the labyrinth, the path of love. The twists and turns are less dramatic this time, but the path is no simpler for that. Slowly his heart is turned from his resentment of God's merciful actions toward the sinful Ninevites. Jonah, nursing his grudge in the punishing sun of the wilderness, is comforted by the shade of the plant that God causes to grow over him. Hot-headed Jonah slowly cools down; the rage slumbering deep in his soul is slowly dispelled. But in the external labyrinth journey, it is the hard internal work that is needed. If Jonah is to complete his path, God's loving nature must be understood and accepted. Once again, Jonah must undergo a painful, life-altering. crisis; once again, he courts death. Yet often truths are grasped only when death is near. Only then can the questions be asked, and the answers found, that lead to the essential turnings. Jonah's heart is turned bit by bit, formed and invited to love.

The final sentence of the whole story seems at first blush to hang in the air like something unfinished; but it's actually extremely profound. It stands like a marker proclaiming the end of the path out of the labyrinth: "And should I not pity Nineveh, that great city, in which there are more than a hundred and twenty thousand persons who do not know their right hand from their left, and also much cattle?"

In these last, jarring words, we see not only the tender humor of love, but the revelation that those who take its path will recognize their bonds, not only to the rest of humanity, but to all of Creation as well.

31

Precious Things Come Slowly

Ariadne's Thread

*To go through a labyrinth
is to set out on a path of transformation.*

The paths of the labyrinth are longest on its outside edge. At the edge you get the feeling that you've lost your way to the center, that you've been shunted aside, destination unknown. These stretches are frustrating and fatiguing. They raise previously unaired questions; those for example, of meaning and meaninglessness.

The path of life sometimes leads us to frontiers where our polite words and beautiful thoughts prove useless. In times of death, sickness, separation, or failure, silence is often preferable to speech, questions to answers. I find that if I'm not directly involved, I try to avoid any contact with people in these situations. Sometimes this distancing takes on a quality of unreality. Death is increasingly removed from our personal experience, it takes place off stage, anonymously, in the hospital. Sickness is hidden when it becomes serious. Separation — from loved ones and family members — is more and more taken for granted these days, so that the pain it causes often goes unrecognized. And failure is simply not discussed in our world of positive thinking.

I'm invited to a men's conference to work with them on the labyrinth. I retell the story of Theseus, which we then act out. Each participant will take a solo journey to the center, equipped with a cord and a sword. Later, we'll share our reflections on the experience. While one of the group is in the labyrinth, the rest of us sit some distance away, under a tree, conversing. One man is long in coming back. When he finally arrives, exhausted, he sits down with us and talks about his adventure.

As he was going into the labyrinth the cord began to get tangled. He made it to the center, stuck his sword into it, and headed back on the return path. After a few minutes he threw the now hopelessly knotted-up cord on the ground in frustration and left the labyrinth. Then he thought about the man who'd be coming next. You couldn't, after all, just leave him a tangled cord. He went back, and slowly and painstakingly untangled the cord.

"Do you know what dawned on me?" he says. "When I separated from my wife, I threw the cord of our relationship on the ground and went off. Now I know that I should have taken the time to untie the knots in it."

Many people abandon the path when it gets difficult. I often observe people in a labyrinth who, when they realize it's taking longer than they'd expected, simply step out over the boundary markers. In this world one is constantly tempted to think that things *have* to go smoothly. Pick out a goal, head off, and you've got it—that's all there is to it. Yet while simple things may come quickly, the precious ones don't. Cures don't come by taking a little pill. A relationship is more than a kiss. Health is not a matter of a "wellness week." And having one spiritual experience doesn't mean that you know God.

Persevering to reach life's real treasures means committing oneself to a difficult path, a path that's neither straight nor short. It's a path that leads through forbidding frontiers, where questions find no easy answers and wastelands make us doubt the meaningfulness of life. It's a path that presents us with an extreme challenge: to open our minds further, to reach toward that greater whole that embraces far more than we can apprehend. If we don't give up at these frontiers, if we don't try to shorten the long paths through these outpost experiences, we will find the turn to the center opening up before us.

32

Doubts about
One's Own Path

Scimangada—Sketch of a city
in the Indian jungle

*Anyone who keeps a foot in the door
won't make any forward progress.*

When I sketch a new labyrinth, I generally begin by laying out the boundaries of the paths. At first everything always looks a little confused. But once I've finished the design, there comes a moment of delight: how clear, how formally beautiful, how complete the whole appears in its finished form. When I'm looking at nature — I'm a biologist — I often have the same experience: so many things appear disordered in their parts, but are revealed to be perfect when seen as a whole.

When I have to make an important decision, I sometimes feel that the labyrinth has nothing to do with the choice before me. I feel overpoweringly that one path is objectively worse; that if I choose wrongly, I'll meet a dead end. If it's a question of some importance, I struggle to come up with all the possible factors that could enter into the equation. Yet once my decision is made, most of the difficulties I'd so anxiously anticipated usually fade away on their own.

A decision always leaves one path untaken. Once I've shaken my lingering indecision and chosen which path to take, I find myself caught up once again in the flow. That path untaken seldom haunts me, but once in a while, I just can't shake the fear that I might have made the wrong choice. It feels like nothing is fitting together, like everything that's come out of the decision has been tough and troublesome. My doubts reassert themselves; I start working the angles on the situation all over again. What did I overlook? What should I have said differently? How can I make things right? Can I reverse my decision, or is it too late? Nothing is more depressing than the sense of having made a wrong decision. Almost as bad is the realization that you've lingered too long in indecision; that you've failed to make any choice at all, and so have let a real opportunity go by.

There are days when all these missed chances and possibly wrong decisions bother me so much that I can hardly think of anything else.

The labyrinth presents a welcome challenge to this sort of irritation, this worriment and second-guessing. Yet when I'm in the middle of weighing a decision, I don't always find myself fully committed to the message of the labyrinth. It seems too simplistic, too out of touch with reality. What the labyrinth says is: Relax, you're on the right path. There *is* no wrong decision. You have to trust. All second-guessing — did I take the right turnoff at the right spot? — is pointless, because there *was* no turnoff. There is only one path for you. Your only choice is to stand still or move on. There is no such thing as a dead end.

But when I'm stuck in self-doubt, I resist the message of the labyrinth. There are, after all, plenty of arguments against it. Surely the labyrinth describes only a part of the truth about life. There have been more than enough bad decisions made throughout history — in fact, made by each one of us — to easily refute the labyrinth's reassuring message.

And yet I also can't dodge its challenge: don't torment yourself, go on, this way is good. There are times when an altogether different feeling comes over me, and the image of the labyrinth leaps before me and says: things are the way they are, and it's good that way. A quiet voice in me responds: What if it's really true? What if every decision in my life *is* good, good and necessary for me to proceed on my path to the center?

I've gotten in the habit of using a little three-word catchphrase: "Suits me fine." Many's the time this has defused a tense situation or ended a crisis for me. It's as if these three little words open a new door. They express the primordial trust that lies in my soul, even when everything seems to speak against it. I am a person with corners and sharp edges; I may make mistakes and errors, but it all "suits me fine." I live in a world that looks like a maze, but actually is a labyrinth.

33

The Face of the Minotaur

Roman floor mosaic in Fribourg, Switzerland

Evil has as much power
as is given to it.

O ne can conceptualize the center of the labyrinth in many ways. It's the goal reached; the Sacred; knowledge; happiness; arrival. But at the center we also find the Minotaur — that which is monstrous, evil. The confrontation with evil cannot be avoided. At the very spot where great and decisive things are being achieved, I also have to confront the question of evil.

Humans are capable of evil. We can decide in favor of evil. We do evil, willingly and unwillingly. We are perhaps the only creatures in the universe capable of that. Usually, the way we deal with this awareness of the potential for evil in ourselves is to project it outward. I myself am the "good hero"; evil is something that exists "out there." Everyone looks for a projection surface on which he or she can make evil visible in some form. Every culture has its projection figures: devils with horns used to do their mischief in the world; now we have fantastic aliens projected, literally, on our television or movie screen. This impulse becomes dangerous, however, when evil is projected no longer onto figures of fantasy, but onto real men and women. It can begin with certain people or groups of people being reviled and labeled as "evil." Sometimes it goes further. Brutish attacks break out and then turn into organized violence. In the attempt to obliterate the evil, these "others" are targeted. It seems that the more violent the attack on the "other"; the greater our blindness toward our own malice. Throughout history, the greatest crimes against humanity have been committed by people who have believed they were combatting evil in the most effective way they knew how. Only later, if at all, did they realize that the evil they sought to purge dwelt with themselves.

The Minotaur in the story of Theseus is the human-devouring creature locked in the center of the labyrinth. It was part man, part bull; an inhuman monster born from the interbreeding of a human and a beast. Humans have always projected onto animals their own offensive and vicious qualities; think of all those terms of abuse we've come up with that apply the names of animals to human. Needless to say, that's being unfair to the animals. The Minotaur, with his bull's head on a human body, is that sort of "bestialized" human. But what the myth is describing here isn't the nature of animals, but rather of humans; it's about recognizing evil in ourselves. Theseus has to confront this monster, and thus himself. He has to look the beast and thus himself, in the eye. Through his struggle with the Minotaur, he conquers himself.

In a labyrinth sketched by Leonardo da Vinci, the center consists of inward facing mirrors linked to form an octagon. By looking into such mirrors one sees oneself from all sides at once. In another mirror labyrinth we find engraved at the center: *This is the Minotaur.* Those who find their way to the center are confronted with the question of evil. That startling sentence tells them to stop seeking evil outside of themselves; they have to look for where it dwells within. This glance at the mirror can be terrifying. But those who refuse to see the evil in themselves remain trapped in their system of projections; and so, paradoxically they're in constant danger of doing evil themselves. The stronger my projection, the less I notice the evil in myself.

This task of self-recognition is extremely hard, and I'm never fully successful. When I do locate the evil in myself, the difficult question arises: how should I now deal with it? Draw my sword and fight? Accept it fatalistically? Or even reconcile with my shadow? No easy answers exist for any of us.

The confrontation with evil is a basic theme of all religions. Christianity sees humans as by nature and from the outset intrinsically entangled in evil. Christ is the savior in the labyrinth of the soul, the one who conquers the Minotaur on our behalf. Complete and unlimited trust in God disarms the power of evil.

The realization of where the confrontation with the power of evil has to take place, and learning how trust in the divine can be continuously acquired, is one of the never-ending tasks of every human being.

34

Turn Around
or You're Trapped

Floor labyrinth in the church of St. Conrad
in Freiburg, Germany

*Readiness for a turnaround
is the prerequisite for progress.*

The labyrinth is a symbol of the turnaround, a change of heart. Inside the labyrinth, one faces two fundamentally different kinds of "turnarounds": First are the regular twists and turns of the path; and then comes the complete turnaround in the center. The turns in the path lead you on your forward way. You change direction, but you don't reverse your progress. Rather, by making a turn you move ahead.

All men and women come to a point in their lives that calls for a wholly new orientation. There's no more continuing in the same direction as before. The path that I've been following is simply at its end. These points can be terribly irritating. Just when I thought I was moving quickly toward the goal, the path suddenly ends. It's as if I've gone the wrong way, as if I've missed the goal. Have I gone so far for nothing? Or maybe I've set a goal for myself, and met with nothing but failure up and down the line. It's hard not to lose one's motivation. Why bother if the whole thing just won't fly? Should I start all over, set out again, continue to march merrily onward? When I try that, my emotions often refuse to "reset." There's a great danger that my disappointment and frustration will bloom into bitterness. And feeling bitter is one of the nastiest things that can happen to a person. To no longer like myself, or others, or anything else — that's one of the worst fates I can imagine.

But many things are more easily said than done. When I've invested all my passion, enthusiasm, and commitment to a path that comes to an abrupt end, it's not at all easy to say: "No big deal, on we go." But the image of the turnaround in the center of the labyrinth gives me the courage to do this: the path doesn't end in a cul-de-sac, but bends and turns into a brand new path.

A turning is not an ending, quite the contrary; many turns lead to the center. It wasn't wrong to have gone this far. Giving up now, resigning yourself to failure — that would be wrong. All the paths are necessary in order to finally reach the center. None of them was pointless or meaningless. All the effort has been repaid. Go into the turn, get out on the path again. This stretch was only a section on

130

your way; it's not yet the goal you originally set out for. This turn in the center of the labyrinth is something different than the turns in the path. Here one is revolving around one's own inner axis. The goal has been reached; the path leads no further, it only leads back. In the labyrinth we find a lot of wisdom and a deep mystery. It's the mystery of the path back.

It's good to set different goals in life and to pursue them; but it's more important to be able to love. The path out of the labyrinth is less spectacular. From the perspective of a world obsessed with expansion, it's even a path of descent, a path on which one no longer pulls off any great achievements. It's a path that men in particular have a hard time taking. They tend to be a little skeptical, to ask "Is this really important?" Not for nothing does Ariadne hand a thread to the hero Theseus so that he can find his path. The path of life is the path down from the towers that you thought you had to build.

If you want to enter the path of life, it will take a fundamental, radical turn at the center.

35

Discovering Oneself
in the Labyrinth

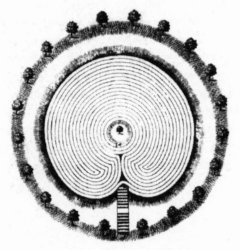

Fortress walk in Slupsk, Poland

*In the labyrinth one begins to track down
the mysteries of one's own life.*

The labyrinth poses the most important life questions. One of these is "What do you want?"

Every decision in life demands that this question be asked. Nothing happens until you've posed and answered it. Even Jesus asks a sick person who comes to him: "Do you want to be made well?" Without inner will there can be no miracles — or at least no possibility of recognizing them when they take place. Sometimes people talk about a great miracle happening to them — while another person, who was on hand to witness it, just shakes her head and smiles. Miracles can be recognized only by those who know precisely what's going on inside of them, who know what they wanted — and what they didn't.

When the miracle happens, a path opens up. This path is not straight, and it is no freeway. Taking it is neither simple nor fast. New turns are always popping up, and with them new questions: "What do I have to give up? What can I leave behind? What's my task now?" These questions always lead into one's interior, where the most important things are at stake.

I can sometimes go through a labyrinth and have nothing happen. But sometimes the whole labyrinth turns into a mirror in which I can fully recognize myself and the particularities of my own current path in life.

The labyrinth is capable of giving that which is inward an outward form. I see, first of all, that I have to set out on a path if I want to reach a goal. I see that turns in the path are unavoidable. Every now and then I harbor a secret hope that I can somehow straighten out a particular turning so that I can avoid having to negotiate it. When I try to do that, I'm brought to an outright halt. I make no headway. I try for a while to use force; then I try to patiently wait it out; but nothing helps. The image of the labyrinth quickly reminds me how unwise it is to try to avoid life's turnings. The only thing that comes of that is stagnation, a standstill.

I once lived in a residence with ex-convicts and pimps. There I met many people who were living on the fringes of society. Their capacities for self-reflection, their abilities to distinguish good from evil, their confrontations with God and the meaning of life, often moved and fascinated me. More than once I got the feeling that they were much farther along on the path to the center than I was.

It can also happen that a walk through the labyrinth raises a particular question that it's time for me to face openly. It could be a question about my past or future, about a career decision or a person with whom I should get in touch. It could be the question: "Can I finally let go of this?" or "What shall I do next?"

I have gone through many labyrinths and had them pose their questions to me. One question comes up more often than any other. It's probably the question with which I struggle the most: "Whom shall I trust?"

36

The Labyrinth
Is a Mirror

Petroglyph in Pontevedra, Spain

*The labyrinth invites us
to discover the beauty of the whole
in all the confusion, imperfection,
and painfulness of life.
It invites us
to set out on the path
with serenity and resolve.
It invites us
to strike out for the center
and to find our way home.*

A labyrinth of lights creates a wonderful atmosphere: gay and mysterious, warm and inviting. I've installed one in a somewhat remote square in the city. A breeze blows through the streets and over the asphalt; sometimes it gathers enough force to extinguish the torches we've set out.

My wife and my father have helped me to light all the little flames. We've just finished. We've hardly noticed the wind, but when we turn around, half the labyrinth has been blown out. Thank God I knew this square and anticipated its wind currents.

That's why I went into a movie house earlier and had them show me popcorn boxes of various sizes.

"I'll need this kind," I told the lady behind the counter.

"One or two?" she asked.

"No, three hundred."

We quickly put each ground torch inside one of the boxes. Barely half an hour later the lights are burning again. Nobody notices the popcorn boxes.

With a labyrinth of lights I always make a path directly out from the center, so that people won't bump trying to pass each other coming and going. People go straight from the entrance to the center and out, again and again. I let them, because, no matter what form it takes, the labyrinth is a mirror. One's experiences in it reflect precisely what's happening in one's own life, or what one needs to know about it.

A woman is standing near me, when a young man strides diagonally across the labyrinth to join his girlfriend, knocking over a torch in the process.

"That's the wrong way!" the lady shouts at the boy.

"No, it's all right," I say. "I imagine that in life he probably climbs over everything conceivable, too. But did you see what the result was? He went past the center. He didn't see it."

136

"What about the people who enter through the exit?" asks someone who's been listening to our conversation.

"Usually you need a long path to get to a goal you've set for yourself. But sometimes you actually can reach your goal very quickly and directly, with no problems. Then again it can take a long path to learn to really appreciate what you reached so easily, or else to get rid of it, to be free again."

On this day I've placed a bowl in the center of the labyrinth containing little cards with sayings on them. As we watch, a man walks directly in from the exit, picks up a card, and takes the exit back out again.

"And what's with him?" the lady asks. I hear her undertone, "*This has to be wrong.*"

"I don't know," I reply. "I only know that he hasn't taken away much from what's lying here right in front of him." And I think to myself that this, too, is probably reflective of his approach to life in general.

I believe that the labyrinth is a masterful tool for self-knowledge—if you allow it to speak to you. Nothing mysterious or magical happens in the labyrinth; it simply makes visible that which was hidden in us.

The labyrinth is our path to the center: a search for life, for the self, and for insight into the mysteries of our existence in this cosmos.

The labyrinth is like an extraordinary wall mirror, which can reflect something of what's moving within me, which shows exactly where I stand. Something of who I am becomes visible.

None of those who come to the labyrinth this day strike me as out of place: not the man who drives by in his car, shouting something; not the one who kneels down, reads a card, and begins to cry; not the ones who enter "the wrong way" and climb out over the barrier; not the ones who have their pictures taken in the center; and not the ones who walk along slowly and thoughtfully, the elderly and the children.

A father turns to me and says, half-apologetically, about his son: "For him, this is nothing." His fourteen-year-old had gotten about halfway through the labyrinth, looking bored; but then he knelt down and spent a long time trying to relight an extinguished torch with a lit one. The father didn't see how much intention and patience his son had shown in rekindling the fire. I can dismiss his effort by saying: "Children just like to light fires." But I could also say: "What a simple, beautiful gesture, to relight the fire when it had gone out."

Even though the labyrinth betrays to an onlooker something about everyone who goes through it — perhaps even about those who choose to pass it by — it will reveal far more to the one who travels its path. Those who look into this mirror can learn a great deal about themselves.

37

Good Questions Are Better
Than Good Answers

Moon labyrinth from a biblical manuscript

*A standpoint
is just a point,
not a universe.*

It's characteristic of a great symbol that it leaves room for many interpretations. For this reason the labyrinth can encompass a wealth of different ideas used for very different purposes.

The long history of the labyrinth has shown this. It was a dancing ground for young people, for brides and grooms, and burial societies; a place to perform the rituals of founding a city and a test of agility performed on horseback at cavalry festivals; a secret place for rites of initiation and a beloved design of mosaic makers. It was used to illustrate books of midwifery, magic, and gardening, as well as Bible manuscripts. It has found its place in churches and bathhouses, marketplaces and town squares, monasteries and banks. I've seen it appear on signs for public projects for women and as a logo for church schools, newspapers, and private forms. The labyrinth has never let itself be monopolized for one specific purpose, and even today it won't be limited. Nor do you find universally applicable answers pronounced by the labyrinths. Good answers are often found, but they'll always be very personal. No two people will walk the same labyrinth to the same effect. A good symbol isn't characterized by the good answers it gives, but rather by the good questions it permits.

I don't think that anyone is against good answers in principle. I myself am a keen seeker of answers. People who have answers have their business taken care of. A person with an answer for every question is satisfied. But when your thirst is gone you don't need to look for the well anymore. Those who don't seek don't find anything. Answers can be like a park bench on which you're comfortably seated. The bench may, in fact, be quite agreeable for the moment, but the view that you have while sitting on it has a rather limited horizon. The rest of the park and the world beyond it remain inaccessible to those who stay on their comfortable answer benches. Having a standpoint is admittedly good and important—but it's also just a point and not a universe.

When the labyrinth poses its challenging question, "Are you going forward or staying put?" not everyone will be ready to answer. Those who are open to new things, who can abandon one point of view and adopt a new one; those who haven't yet found what they're looking for, who have more good questions than answers, will likely choose the forward path.

140

38

An Archetypal
Image of Life

Modern Christian labyrinth

*In the labyrinth you don't lose yourself,
you find yourself.*

— Hermann Kern

The labyrinth is an archetypal image of life, a mirror of the soul. In the labyrinth I rediscover myself on my path through life. At birth I'm invited to enter upon this path. I'm led to turnings and challenges in order to persevere through them, equipped with an unquenchable longing for the center. I'm led to the center yet forced to turn away from it again and again in order to move ahead. I experience desolate frontiers and doubts and the recurrent feeling that this path will never get me anywhere. Nevertheless the center holds me fast; it won't let me fall out of its orbit.

On my path I meet others; sometimes I walk along with them for a while, and then I'm alone again. Sometimes I follow the crowd, sometimes I go against the flow. Sometimes I completely lose sight of someone, only to meet him or her again by surprise. Sometimes I need a helping hand to manage a difficult curve; sometimes an overzealous companion pulls me off the road.

There are times when the path becomes a dance, and I feel like singing; at other times I'm consumed by impatience. Sometimes a little shiver takes hold of me when — usually, to my surprise — the path opens up to the center.

The center is a wondrous place. It shelters and protects, brings joy and comfort. I draw from the source; I'm linked to all of humanity, the whole universe. It's a profoundly good place to be. But at some point I know that it isn't all there is. I have to go back if I am to complete the experience. This path out of the labyrinth has a different quality, an uncluttered clarity that belongs to it alone. Far fewer impressions and words punctuate the journey home. It's a wonderful path, a precious path, a silent path, almost so silent that one doesn't want to speak of it.

The labyrinth is a sacred tool for knowing; an image that connects us to God, the world, and ourselves. There is something of mystery in it, and at the same time a fascinating clarity and perfection. It reveals something of our mysterious being to ourselves and offers us a glimpse of the beauty and harmony of the universe in which we are cradled.

List of
Illustrations

All illustrations are by Gernot Candolini, except:

Chapters 2 and 13: from Robert Field, *Mazes, Ancient and Modern* (Norfolk, England: Tarquin Publications, 1999).

Chapter 5: from W. H. Matthew, *Mazes and Labyrinths* (London: Longmans, Green & Co., 1922).

Chapter 9: Adrian Fisher, *www.labyrinti.com*.

Chapters 10, 15, 23, 28, and 33, and the drawing on p. 16: Jeff Saward — Caerdroia, *www.labyrinthos.net*.

Chapter 11: Leonardo da Vinci in the facsimile volume of the Reale Commissione Vinciana, vol. 5 (Rome, 1941); reproduced in Hermann Kern, *Labyrinthe* (Munich: Prestel-Verlag, 1982).

Chapter 12: from Nicholas R. Mann, *Glastonbury Tor* (Glastonbury: Annenterprise, 1986).

Chapters 26–27, 30, and 36–37: from Carl Schuster and Edmund Carpenter, *Patterns That Connect* (New York: The Rock Foundation, 1996).

Chapter 29: from Hermann Hugo, *Die christliche Seele im Labyrinth der Welt* (Antwerp, 1632); reproduced in Hermann Kern, *Labyrinthe* (Munich: Prestel-Verlag, 1982).

About the Author

Gernot Candolini has studied and taught biology, worked as a youth director in the church, and is now a renowned author, photographer, and architect of labyrinths. As a part of his work with labyrinths he trains church leaders in the use of the labyrinth as a tool in personal spiritual growth and practice. Since 1992 Gernot has been studying the history and design of labyrinths in many countries and from many cultures. He communicates that knowledge in books, lectures, and training seminars. Gernot lives with his family in Innsbruck.

Many photographs illustrative of the journey and experiences described in this book may be found in the coffee-table book *Das geheimnisvolle Labyrinth: Mythos und Geschichte eines Menschheitssymbols* (Pattloch, 1999).

Anyone who would like to engage in practical work with labyrinths will find an introduction, suggestions, and useful materials in: *Labyrinthe: Ein Praxisbuch zum Malen, Bauen, Tanzen, Spielen, Meditieren und Feiern* (Pattloch, 1999).

You can find Gernot Candolini's homepage at *www.labyrinthe.at.*